# THE MARRIAGE ACT

THE RISK I TOOK TO KEEP MY BEST FRIEND IN AMERICA . . .
AND WHAT IT TAUGHT US ABOUT LOVE

## LIZA MONROY

Soft Skull Press
an imprint of Counterpoint, Berkeley

Photo on page 293 by Kimberly Buchheit. Photo on page 296 by Judi Warehouse. All other personal photos are courtesy of the author's private collection. Every effort has been made to trace or contact all other copyright holders. The publishers will be pleased to make good any omissions or rectify any mistakes brought to their attention at the earliest opportunity.

Library of Congress Cataloging-in-Publication Data
Monroy, Liza.
The marriage act : the risk I took to keep my best friend in America, and what it taught us about love / Liza Monroy.
pages cm
ISBN 978-1-59376-536-1
1. Marriage—United States. 2. Matrimonial actions—United States. 3. Marriage law—United States. 4. Intercountry marriage—United States. 5. Aliens—United States. 6. Gay men—Relations with heterosexual women I. Title.
HQ536.M545 2014
306.810973—dc23
2013028275

Interior design by Sabrina Plomitallo-González, Neuwirth & Associates
Cover design by Jennifer Heuer

Soft Skull Press
An Imprint of Counterpoint
1919 Fifth Street
Berkeley, CA 94710
www.softskull.com

Printed in the United States of America
Distributed by Publishers Group West

10 9 8 7 6 5 4 3 2 1

For Emir

# Author's Note

"Memory is in this respect similar to anticipation: an instrument of simplification and selection."
—Alain de Botton, *The Art of Travel*

"Reality is the child of man's imagination."
—Frigyes Karinthy, *A Journey Round My Skull*

One of the challenges in telling any personal story is reconciling faithfulness to fact with the subjective nature of individual perception. Sometimes, imagination invades even the surest of memories.

In this work, details of some events and identities have been changed in order to protect privacy, prevent deportation, and minimize the likelihood of anyone's arrest.

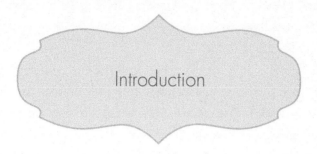

# Introduction

Offering my hand in marriage to my close friend Emir had nothing to do with civil rights issues the night I got down on one knee in a crowded West Hollywood gay bar. I didn't do it as activism or to make a statement. Even though this act of marriage came to have political meaning in the aftermath, making a political gesture was not my intent. That came later. At the time, I proposed out of love, empathy, and support, along with desperation to keep Emir with me. All of it was done in secret. With a handful of exceptions, I didn't talk about it, and I certainly never imagined I would write a book "coming out" about it because our story had a place in a national conversation about equality, or that our story could further reveal the illogical underpinnings of why a debate ever existed in the first place.

At first, the story of Emir and me sounded mostly like a premise for one of the Hollywood movies I spent my days working on then, in my early twenties: Lost-but-Optimistic Young Woman

Marries Her Gay Best Friend—who is from a Muslim family in the Middle East—to keep him in the country, while her mother works for the State Department preventing immigration fraud. I used to refer to Emir and me as "Will and Grace on steroids," but when gender-neutral marriage grew from niche to national issue in 2004, as Mayor Gavin Newsom of San Francisco began issuing marriage licenses to same-sex couples, I realized that what I had taken to calling "the book about us" went beyond a romantic comedy with a catchy premise. Marrying Emir was, as with any marriage-type thing, a purely personal decision. Then again, The Personal Is Political and all.

When I decided to write about us, I thought I was writing a book about friendship. After all, what sustains the core of marriage if not friendship? But as I began writing, larger questions came to preoccupy me: What defines a union? What *is* a marriage? How can there be "correct" and "incorrect" love? Who is to say which loves are valid—valuable—and which are not? In writing *The Marriage Act*, I realized this personal narrative could highlight the absurdities of our marriage laws. How, in this century, is there still debate about gender discrimination? What it boils down to is that there are still second-class citizens in the United States today, and until gender-neutral marriage is legal federally, there will continue to be.

The irony is that while technically Emir and I fit into the proper gender classification of DOMA, The Defense of Marriage Act—which defined marriage as between one man and one woman—our marriage was, in actuality, less "conventional," less "traditional," than Emir's partnership with his true love, Stan (and the "traditional" familial love of millions of same-sex couples). It all leads to quite the quandary over the definition of marriage, and the absurdity of not granting federal marriage benefits to same-sex couples.

And yet, on another level, Emir and I *were* real. The surface reasons our marriage was illegitimate were that its main driving force was immigration, and that he is gay and I knew it when I married him. I wanted to marry him in spite of these things as much as because of them; even though I popped the question because he stood to be deported otherwise, even though he was gay, *I wanted to marry him anyway.* Marriage springs from emotion and emotions aren't rational. With our history, deep emotional bond, and love of each other, Emir and I shared everything except sex. This blurry line came to highlight the ironies and problems of forbidding gender-neutral marriage on the federal level, of denying tens of thousands of couples the benefits that federal marriage provides—immigration of a foreign-born partner in particular—solely based on the couple being the same sex rather than opposite sexes. Now that DOMA has been done away with and Proposition 8 along with it, it looks as though the path has been cleared more so than before, but until same-sex marriage is federally recognized and available in every state, there is still a ways to go.

After the uproar leading to Proposition 8 resulted in nation-wide attention to the debate over gender-neutral marriage, immigration entered the picture. Even in the fifteen states (as of this writing) where same-sex marriage is legal, if one partner is a U.S. citizen but not the other, the citizen is powerless to keep his or her partner in the country should the partner lose the legal ability to stay by other means, such as an H-1B work visa.

Same-sex marriages are invisible on the federal level. So while I could marry Emir or even a man off the street and secure him a green card, couples with more "traditional" marriages—monogamy and life devotion and even children—have been powerless to do the same. The consequences are devastating.

One such case was that of Bradford Wells and Anthony John Makk, a couple for nineteen years and counting. Makk is Australian and Wells is a U.S. citizen with health complications from AIDS. Makk, his caregiver, was threatened with deportation after being denied spousal immigration benefits, even though the couple lived in Massachusetts, where same-sex marriage is legal, because of DOMA—which Bill Clinton signed into law in 1996, and which defined marriage on the federal level as existing solely between one man and one woman.

"At first," the *San Francisco Chronicle* wrote, "[Wells and Makk] said, they were fighting only for themselves, but now feel they represent all of the estimated 36,000 binational same-sex couples who are barred from spousal immigration benefits."

Wells and Makk were far from alone. Melanie Servetas, a banking executive who fell in love with a Brazilian woman, could not sponsor her partner to come to the United States, as straight people can with a fiancé visa, even for mail-order brides. Servetas gave up her career and life in the United States to be with her partner. The choice comes down to love or country, and, as lawyer Brandon Perlberg, who moved to London to be with his partner, put it, "you don't get more committed than giving up your country."

Fortunately, the marriage of Wells and Makk can now be recognized. In an age where pseudo-celebrities like Kim

Kardashian marry for publicity and reality shows pull marriage-related stunts, yet a terminally ill man must struggle to keep the love of his life in the country with him, the need for universal marriage equality is more evident than ever. This isn't a "gay issue." It's a human rights issue. And all of us—gay, straight, and anything in between or otherwise—have a stake. These, too, are the stakes behind this story, and stories are our most important tools in effecting change.

That my mother was, as Emir dubbed her (always with emphasis), *an immigration person* who worked for a living preventing the very thing we were doing brought up questions of family, loyalty, and doing the right thing even if it means betraying that which sustained you. Fortunately, compassion and love are starting to win out. Before the Supreme Court repealed DOMA in 2013, Bill Clinton admitted regret for ever signing it into law. And David Blankenhorn, founder and president of the conservative group Institute for American Values who was an "expert witness" in favor of Proposition 8, recently wrote in the *Los Angeles Times*, "I changed my opposition to gay marriage because of personal relationships. . . . The key was the gradual breakthrough of empathy."

That's what this is ultimately about—devotion and empathy. My devotion to keeping Emir with me took priority above doing what my mother would have wanted and above my country's laws. It was worth taking any risk to keep Emir with me, and that alone showed me the true nature of our relationship: we already were family. We needed to make that official so he could stay in Los Angeles, where we both wanted him, and that's the ultimate Marriage Act: motivated by love, companionship, and support. In retrospect, and with marriage and immigration rights in the headlines, my union to Emir remains—as true marriages are—an act of devotion. That is why this book, my contribution to the conversation, takes the form of a love story.

# Part I:
# Seeking Asylum

# 1.

## Vacancy

No matter what, you could count on a glorious day in Los Angeles. The perpetual lull of cars passing on the boulevard outside the bedroom window, soothing as the sound of the ocean: constant, steady, and rhythmic. That December, the weather seemed the one constant in a time when recounts and pregnant chads dominated headlines and KCRW, the local NPR station I listened to obsessively. The Supreme Court was about to declare George W. Bush the country's forty-third president and we still had no idea what we were in for. And by "we" I mean the world, the country, and the microscopic piece of it all that was Emir and me. I had just turned twenty-one. All of it still lay ahead of us.

One late afternoon at Emir's poolside apartment in West Hollywood, during the period after college when we were both underemployed, he handed me a steaming cup of sweet, milky tea and I told him about the embarrassing ritual I'd developed. It entailed sitting for hours on my bedroom floor rereading Julian's old love letters, letters I imagined him scrawling when he was bored in morning meetings at Big Wall Street Investment Bank and on the countless cross-country flights he took to see me. I combed through these letters again and again, trying to figure out what I had missed.

I'd dreamed of marrying Julian since I was sixteen. We met in high school in Mexico City. Five years later, we got engaged while in a long-distance, bicoastal relationship. Two weeks before I was supposed to leave Los Angeles to live with Julian in New York, our relationship imploded. Julian was reduced to a little pile of letters.

"Do you want me to keep them in my filing cabinet for you?" Emir offered.

"I'd just come over here even more and keep reading them."

"Then there's only one solution."

Emir led the letters and me downstairs to the building's subterranean carport. We crouched over a drain in the concrete, a pose of genuflection. He held the first one out over the drain while I lit the match. The flare illuminated his dark eyes, flickering shadows across our faces. Julian—paper Julian—blew away in the breeze of a warm Santa Ana.

"You don't have to be stuck in the past," Emir said. "There's so much more out there for you."

Once upon a time there were three important men in my life. Julian and my father were gone. And there was Emir, right where he always was, right in front of me, in plain sight.

I first laid eyes on Emir al-Habibi when he walked into the advanced film production classroom in black-and-white Adidas workout pants and gym shoes. He had cute, curly dark hair, full pillow lips, and a broad white smile that took over his face. He could have passed for any average American college kid, though his face, with tan skin and dark, dramatic features, would have been perfectly cast in a Benetton ad. He was Mediterranean or Middle Eastern. I was struck by how familiar he looked until I realized he resembled . . . me. He could have been my long-lost fraternal twin. When we had to form groups for short film projects during class, we both stood and drifted toward each other as if we already knew we were somehow linked, or meant to be. At Emerson College in Boston, Emir was an international student and I felt like one. This was the subject of one of our earliest conversations:

"During orientation, someone asked me if back home I rode around on a camel," Emir said. "And I told him, 'Someone's seen *Aladdin* too many times.'"

I laughed. "I've been asked if in Mexico City I rode to school on a burro."

"Someone's seen *The Three Caballeros* too many times."

I was immediately drawn to this kindred spirit. We each spoke three languages and were living in the United States for the first time. (Emir more so than me. I was born in Seattle but left when I was five.) We loved travel, film, shopping, and dancing. It was a typical personal-ad list of leisure activities, but when we were together, even the mundane took on an air of adventure. We were idealists, optimists, and as Emir phrased it, "love-fools." We both wanted to be screenwriters. Emir was already on his way: his romantic drama about a middle-aged divorcée who inherits a hotel in Egypt from an eccentric aunt became a finalist in a national screenplay competition, while I stuffed my earliest effort, a pretentious piece about a painter, a Greek professor, and Jean-Paul Sartre, into the recesses of a very dark desk drawer.

Emir and I made our first film together that first semester. I'd adapted a William S. Burroughs short story called "The Junky's Christmas." The protagonist, the forlorn junky, gives the shot of heroin that took all day to score to a kid moaning in pain in the next room at the motel where he goes to shoot up. The Kid, who has a kidney stone, is soothed by the opiate and can finally rest. After giving up the drug he worked so hard to get, the Junky returns to his room dismayed, only to suddenly find himself inexplicably, completely high. It's the immaculate fix, the elevation that comes from doing a good deed with nothing expected in return. Emir and I had no idea how strongly that metaphor would return, how much more it would come to mean.

Everything went seamlessly during production on *The Junky's Christmas*. The script was tight, the story funny, and our actors hit every beat. We were so proud the day it was in the can, we called it "our baby." But when we went to pick up the print from the film-processing lab, we were horrified to find our baby was stillborn: an undetectable light leak in the camera had overexposed the film. There was no way we could have known, the technician told us—as if knowing it wasn't our fault might lessen the blow. We had been so confident we never anticipated it could end in disaster. After finding out, we sat side by side on my futon not saying a word. It was the first time we cried over something that should have been beautiful gone terribly wrong.

Marriage hunger wasn't new to me. After four years back in the United States, I still couldn't shake the feeling of being overseas. It was the opposite of Dorothy's saying, "There's no place like home"—no place was. The only constant was change. I was barely twenty-one, but completely convinced I needed to settle down and start creating the nuclear family I never had. In opposition to peers who sought adventure, independence, and freedom, I wanted to live in one place, put down roots, and experience predictability.

My parents divorced when I was six, during my mother's first tour with the U.S. State Department in Guadalajara, Mexico. My mother and I, her only child, moved around every few years to different countries for her government job. I was naturally independent but also lonely.

I lived alone in the summer of 1996, at sixteen: the summer Julian and I became inseparable. My mother had moved a few blocks away from our house in Lomas de Chapultepec, and in with her boyfriend, Harvey. She had gotten me a job in the visa section of the U.S. Embassy downtown, and picked me up for work in the morning. Evenings, she dropped me back off at our house before continuing on to Harvey's. A high school girlfriend came back to Mexico to visit from Russia, where her family had moved, and stayed with me for a few weeks. One afternoon she announced she was going to the flea market with another friend of hers, Julian. We had our first date a few days later, to Plaza Coyoacán in the south of the city, where we sipped tequila and *sangrita* at a bar called El Hijo del Cuervo and stayed up all night talking. I had no idea what we were, or what we would become, but even then my feelings for Julian were mysterious, different from the teenage crushes I'd had before. As I hugged him good-bye that night, I inhaled the scent of his leather jacket, rested my head on his chest, and thought: *I am going to marry him.* I went upstairs and giggled at the absurdity of the idea that, in high school, one could find the person they would spend the rest of their life with.

Julian was over six feet tall—a bear of a man, like my father, from when I could remember him—with large, intense green eyes. Though girls adored him, he was shy and said he hardly dated in high school. He spent most of his time with his rowdy, unconventional group of friends: flannel-wearing, pierced, Harvard- and MIT-bound innovator-kids. His mother was a Swiss divorcée who had been married to a Mexican—Julian's father, a brilliant engineer who was also unstable. During high school, Julian lived with his mother in Polanco, a popular shopping neighborhood; its main drag, Avenida Presidente Masaryk, was Mexico City's equivalent of Rodeo Drive. While most of our classmates had lavish homes, their apartment was small.

Our connection felt fated. As would later happen with Emir,

Julian and I had uncanny commonalities. I had been rootless since my mother joined the Foreign Service when I was five and we became members of a class the writer Pico Iyer dubs the "privileged homeless." Julian grew up this way, too, moving between Mexico, Switzerland, and New York City. He also carried passports from two countries, spoke three languages, and was the only child of a domineering single mother who moved a lot. Our fathers spent more time with the bottle than with us, though Julian's father was an ambitious career man and notorious womanizer, while mine was a quiet waiter who rarely dated, saying my mother and I were his family.

But there was another side to Julian, a part of him I could neither access nor understand. This was the part that was not kind, the part with the terrible insomnia, the part that complained of nightmares and disappeared for days on end. During his disappearances, I lay on my bedroom carpet, paralyzed until he called or showed up at the gate. Like my father, he never explained the absence, and at sixteen I was afraid that bringing it up would mean losing him for good. Every time, I welcomed him back, no questions asked. Over the course of our first summer this became a pattern. I wouldn't hear from him for days before he resurfaced. When he did, I acted as if nothing had happened and everything was fine. I didn't have a gauge or model for a healthy relationship. What was clear was that Julian had a tendency to disappear, much like the other man (not) in my life.

Julian and I stayed in touch on and off after he moved to the States on a full scholarship to an Ivy League university. We dated other people until we reunited when Emir and I were juniors at Emerson, in 1999. Julian was working as an investment banker in New York; we traded weekends between our two cities, joking that we single-handedly funded Amtrak and the Greyhound bus.

I was already signed up to spend my last semester, September to December of 2000, in Los Angeles, at Emerson's West Coast campus. So was Emir, who had secured an internship with a powerful producer at a big movie studio. We would take our final courses in advanced screenwriting and independent production from the Hollywood insiders teaching Emerson's West Coast classes. Emir and I had both accumulated enough credits (taken over summers we preferred spending in Boston to going "home") to graduate in December, a semester ahead of schedule. Emir hoped to parlay his internship into an entry-level studio job as a development assistant or glorified secretary. After I graduated, Julian and I agreed, I would move to New York and we would be together for the rest of our lives. He flew out to visit me in L.A. every other weekend; with his Wall Street job, he could afford to. In L.A., I interned at a small production company and gave Emir driving lessons.

"I'm really afraid to get on the highway," he said. "Will you be in the car when I get on the highway?"

"They call it the freeway here. And sure—I'll help with whatever you need."

In October, Julian proposed. Or rather, he slid a diamond ring on my finger in the dark while I was half-asleep, but no matter—I was engaged to the man I had fantasized about marrying since I was a teenager. For a diplomat's kid who had never lived in the same country for longer than four years, it seemed nothing short of a miracle. As soon as Julian left for the airport on Sunday, I ran to Emir's building, the next one over from mine in the corporate complex (the M to my L), and showed him the ring. "You're getting married!" he said as we danced around his studio, which was an exact replica of mine.

While friends were deciding what city to live in with roommates, barhopping, hooking up, and interviewing for first jobs, I was moving to New York City to assume my next identity: young Wall Street wife. The notion of stability thrilled me. I knew exactly how my life was going to go. Julian and I would live in a comfortable apartment in Manhattan, and I would accompany him on business trips to London and Paris, where I would write screenplays in hotel rooms while he went to meetings. We would eat in the best restaurants and sip delicious cocktails. My visions stopped short of purse dogs and Hermès bags because Julian and I were more down-to-earth, the way my mother raised me: don't be showy. Chase experiences, as material things are of little value. My mother adored Julian. He fit exactly her idea of the man her daughter should end up with: successful, ambitious, international, hyper-educated.

Someone unlike the man she had chosen for herself, a man no longer in either of our lives.

I reveled in the notion that now, for as long as we both would live, Julian and I could look at each other and say, "Remember when . . ."—a phrase I could not share with anyone else but my mother. My words turned into fodder for her worries: Would I be able to make a living? Did I know how to be a proper judge of character and balance my checkbook? Was I too trusting and naïve? Would I succeed or disappoint? Did I drink too much? Was I going to the dentist? She fostered concerns the way I kept journals: obsessively. When I was younger, I wrote to release frustration and anger I couldn't voice. I was the only child and the ultimate project. I wouldn't tell my mother I had a tattoo (Julian, a closeted artist, had designed a depiction of our linked initials that we had inked in hidden places), much less that I was fired from a job. Even a hint of my mother's disappointment made my stomach clench. I complained about this to Emir. "You have a Jewish mummy," he said. "My father's the same way with me even though he's a man and Muslim."

"We aren't as different as we like to think," Emir said.

Emir had to hide his real identity ever since realizing what it meant: that loving someone of the same gender was unnatural, against God's will, and deserving of punishment. In West Hollywood, he walked down the street holding hands with his then-boyfriend, Adrian. Where Emir was from, if it became suspected he had a sexual relationship with another man, he would be killed.

Emir grew up gay in a Muslim country. Specifically which, to protect his identity, I promised him I wouldn't say, and so I'll refer to this place as Emiristan, the gay-intolerant land he waited all his young life to flee. He hid who he really was from his father, an image-obsessed businessman. His mother guessed the truth. She had her suspicions and confronted him the week before he moved to Boston. Emir didn't confirm or deny it. He just stood there in the kitchen as his mother cried and asked him to please never tell his father, who would surely divorce her. *Divorce HER?* As if it was her fault? "It's the mentality," Emir said. "My sisters don't know either. When I was in high school, I saw on the news about gays being murdered and left by the side of the highway. I knew that if I stayed I would always be one of those married fathers who still go looking for boys online and in street corners and by tapping their feet under airport bathroom stalls, fooling myself and not living my life."

I behaved with my mother as Emir did with his father. We hid who we really were in favor of more "acceptable" personas, but Emir's dilemma had higher stakes: people in Emiristan suspected to be gay have been beaten with metal pipes, had their genitals cut off, and been stabbed and left to die in ditches. This happened to Amir, one of two other young gay men Emir knew in high school, while we were in college. *I told him to stay away from Dunkin' Donuts*, Emir said in the aftermath; the same innocuous franchised coffee shop in the basement of our Boston dorm was one of the few gay cruising spots in

Emiristan's capital. *But who was I to talk, I used to hang out there too. It could have been me.* Emir swore he would never go home again but it was an impossible promise to keep. His family lived there. He had to see them. My situation wasn't life-or-death like Emir's, but I understood what it felt like to pretend to be someone you're not for somebody else.

My latest plan did satisfy my mother: move in with the investment banker she approved of and start a career in New York. As far as worlds went, it appeared I was on top of mine, what with the diamond ring, Julian-fiancé, and my twenties spread ahead of me, an open road as improbably perfect as the 405 without traffic. So why did my eyes still dart around suspiciously, fearful of the edge of the cliff sneaking up? And why did the engagement ring look and feel so foreign on my finger, as if the hand belonged to someone else? What would I be missing by not experiencing that in-between stage after college, when people did things like going out dancing all night and rolling into work at seven with the energy to put in a full day, or creating budget spreadsheets to figure out whether one could survive on grocery store sushi, frozen yogurt, and red wine?

With three weeks until my move, I mentioned to Julian I was having doubts, that I was afraid I might not be ready. He coldly told me to stay in L.A. He said it quickly, which I took to mean he had been feeling the same way. That minute-long phone call turned out to be the full extent of discussion about the nondecision to end our engagement. I was devastated, though I shouldn't have been surprised. Julian had told me before of his

ability to cut people out of his life—he snapped his fingers—
"like that."

Emir had already signed a lease on an apartment with a roommate in West Hollywood. If he hadn't, he said, of course he
would have wanted to live with me. I started looking for an
apartment with my closest college girlfriends, Jen and Kate, who
had been best friends since meeting as kids in a small Massachusetts town. They did everything together, including driving
Kate's mother's breaking-down burgundy minivan across the
country from Boston to Los Angeles. Some who didn't know
them mistook them for a couple, which we laughed about.
Boys were what we spent most of our time talking about: boys
we loved, boys we wished loved us, boys we wanted, boys who
broke our hearts. It was all about the boys. None of us had
fathers or, for that matter, really any men in our immediate
families. I had no siblings, and Jen and Kate had sisters. We were
starved for male attention. Being aware of this didn't help us
change it, at least not at that point in our lives.

Just like that, I lived in another home that wasn't.

A few days later, my mother swept down from the sky. She informed me I was moving to Athens, Greece, where she had been stationed since the year I started college, to live with her. She would get me a job at the U.S. Embassy. She was trying to take me back.

"You can't move me around anymore," I said.

When my mother realized I wasn't going anywhere, Jen and Kate and I found an apartment in West Hollywood that was upstairs from a couple of junkies. My mother got busy fixing everything. This, too, was part of her job: managing other people's crises. She hightailed it to Ikea, to the Volkswagen dealership, to the grocery store, as if she was running down a checklist. Emir came over to help her build the furniture while Jen and Kate job-searched and I worked as a freelance receptionist at a production company.

When the furniture was built and car insurance procured, my mother returned to Athens and left us three underemployed girls in West Hollywood to our own devices. I continued my receptionist gig at the production company. Anxious to prove myself, I thought that was the answer: that creating a successful career would both satisfy my mother and fill a void I felt so strongly I'd given it a name, The Lack.

Julian sent a message via his secretary asking for the ring back. He wanted me to FedEx it and send him the tracking number. One hot, smoggy afternoon, Jen and Kate drove around with me to pawnshops, where I sought appraisals instead (money was suddenly short), but I couldn't bring myself to sell it. In the end, Emir accompanied me to the post office, where I mailed it back certified. The little green ticket arrived a week later, confirming its receipt, and that was it. Everything felt empty and strange. With no more fiancé and no real career prospects, I was back to being . . . twenty-one.

Emir and I were neighbors again, this time three blocks away from each other in West Hollywood. It was rare to be able to walk to visit a friend in Los Angeles. Emir worked from sunup to midnight in his internship for the powerful studio producer. On his rare days off, I sat on the couch in his immaculate, white, light-filled apartment, where we talked for hours. Compared to my messy, chaotic abode with its pink Hello Kitty appliances, Emir's place felt like another world: a place of organization, order, and calm. I went there to unwind while Emir played Sims or read screenplays for work.

Aside from film sets where I would eventually work in the art department, driving all over L.A. looking for decorative objects that would illuminate a character or set a certain tone, I would spend the year ahead on the hunt for a replacement huge, impossible, ridiculous, soul-consuming, all-encompassing love. Finding that love, I imagined, would justify losing Julian, because there was something else I was supposed to do, or someone else I was supposed to marry.

Emir understood.

"We're love-fools," he reminded me. "Fool being the key word."

As much as I wished it were otherwise, I agreed.

Jen, Kate, and I lived in the apartment above the junkies for most of that first year in L.A. Jen and Kate were waitressing and dating. I was asleep by the time they brought the party home when the bars closed. I woke up at four or five in the morning to go work on sets. *I can do anything from here. I am free, truly free. So I better find something useful, something worthwhile, something good to do with my freedom.*

I heard from my father for the first time in three years. A postcard—a baffling postcard—arrived from Italy. The image: Portofino, boats in the harbor. The words amounted to some kind of Dadaist poetry.

> HERE I AM BACK HOME.
> FLYTH WAS MARVELOUS!
> NONNA DOING GREAT!
> AND ALL IN THE FAMILY!
> I FEEL GREAT AND HAPPY
> TO START A NEW LIFE
> IN GENOVA!!
> CONGRATULATION FOR
> YOURS NEW CAREER!! AND
> WISHING YOU MY VERY BEST!!
> LOVE DAD!

The postcard didn't explain a thing, other than that he had returned to Italy. If anything, it increased the mystery. My father always said Seattle was his home. Why would he move to Italy without telling anyone? Nonna was in her nineties, my mother explained, so he must have wanted to go take care of her. The explanation reeked of covering up something else. Even when my father resurfaced he remained in the shadows.

He was influential even in his absence, that is, the absence itself became a trigger. It set me up perfectly on this quest for stability, of which finding a husband was Step One.

Toward the end of the summer of 2001, I was considering moving to New York in an attempt to undo what I'd come to see as the biggest mistake of my life. Emir had gone on a week-long trip to the City to visit a childhood friend, and his being there got me thinking about Julian. *Look! It took me a while, but I'm here now!* I would say. I could try to put things back together the way they should have been to begin with, follow the initial plan, which I believed more and more strongly would have been the right one. I drew tarot cards on my bedroom floor that night, seeking guidance from some greater force.

*Stay in California?*

*Move to New York?*

The next morning, the downstairs neighbor woke Jen, Kate, and me with agitated pounding on our front door. My boss on the movie called. Work was cancelled until further notice. My mother called. My father didn't. Nobody knew what was going on, or the scope of it. There could be planes in the air headed for the skyscrapers in downtown L.A. for all we knew. *Stay inside. Watch the news.* Would we have to evacuate the city? In the hours of aftermath, no one knew anything yet.

Emir. His childhood friend, El Toro, lived in Park Slope. Had they gone into Manhattan that morning? Emir had told me before he left that he would visit the World Trade Center one of his days there for a leisurely breakfast at Windows on the World. By late afternoon I was able to reach the two people I knew who lived in New York: Julian, who walked from his Midtown office to his apartment on the Upper East Side and after reporting that he was fine, hadn't been anywhere near it, promptly hung up the phone; and my Great-Uncle Vance, my mother's father's brother, who lived in Chelsea and had seen the towers fall from the roof of his building. I could not reach Emir. For hours after I turned on the news that morning at the crack of dawn, I worried about another missing man I loved. I dialed his number over and over. The whole world had changed in an instant, and simply being Middle Eastern was cause for being detained in Brooklyn's Metropolitan Detention Center and held indefinitely. And so we came to the place where my story ended and ours began.

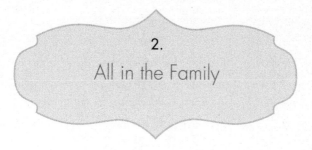

## 2.
## All in the Family

In Los Angeles, homemade banners around town declared, WE ARE ALL AMERICANS NOW. Sun pounded down through the smog, refracting off windshields. Cloudless sky, temperature in the seventies. Traffic crept along palm tree–lined streets. September was a beautiful month in Southern California, heat of summer fading, sunlight soft as if a cinematographer were lighting a scene that called for an ethereal mood. Nothing looked any different, yet everything had changed. Recent history would now be divided into before and after.

On the day that flights resumed, I stood in the chaos of the Remote Cell Phone Waiting Lot at LAX. No one was allowed near the terminals. All of us gawked at the seemingly banal sight of aircraft circling overhead. For two days, the skies had been empty. Emir's return reservation was moved to one of the first flights to leave New York City. I worried that he could have been taken aside for questioning at the airport based on his looks or the nationality listed on his passport. Middle Eastern men were being detained without grounds.

Relief washed over me as Emir climbed out of one of the vans. He waved, pulling his rolling suitcase through the crowd. I pushed forward until we reached each other. We hugged for what felt like a very long time, his familiar smell of CK One and cigarette smoke a relief. When he removed his aviator sunglasses, I saw the dark circles that rimmed his eyes. Emir typically had a goatee or five o'clock shadow, but that day his coffee-colored skin was clean-shaven, making him appear teenaged.

"People were looking at me weird on the plane."

"People aren't that prejudiced."

"They will be now."

"Emir," I said. "No one would ever mistake *you* for a terrorist."

"Yeah, terrorists wouldn't let me join up with them even if I wanted to. They would go all Red Queen on me, *off with his head.*"

We walked across the lot and got into my little red Golf. I merged into traffic on strip-club-and-car-rental-company-lined Airport Boulevard. From the driver's seat I saw him in my peripheral vision. He stared out the window into the distance as traffic rushed by. The freeway still made him nervous but now so did a host of other things.

Emir rolled down the window, lit two cigarettes, and passed me one. I took it even though I was quitting. Warm air and smoke whipped through the car. Complaining that his lips were dry from stale cabin air, he reached into his backpack for his ChapStick but pulled out a thin metal tube instead.

"Shit. I completely forgot I had this."

"What is that?" I asked.

"Mace."

"*Mace?* What are you doing with mace in your bag?"

"I forgot. I always carried it, an old habit from fearing gay-bashers back home."

It surprised us both that two days after terrorists used mace to hijack aircraft, no screener caught the canister in Emir's backpack; but more frightening was what might have happened if they had.

He found the ChapStick and slicked a glossy layer onto his full lips. I sped up and merged on the 405, the little red car dwarfed by a swarm of SUVs.

I remember the citrus salads and late-afternoon Cosmopolitans in the sunny outdoor courtyard of the Abbey, our favorite West Hollywood gay bar. I remember how strange it felt to walk to his apartment rather than drive even though he lived only three blocks away from me. I can't remember the precise instance when Emir first brought up the verging-on-problematic visa situation. It might have been at a sushi restaurant, or over lunches at the Abbey, or while in line at what the boys around the neighborhood called "the gay Starbucks" on Santa Monica. Emir wanted to stay in the United States past this year to avoid going back into the closet in Emiristan and living with his father. In order to stay, he had to find a job before his visa expired in December, a year after graduation. I told him I was sure he'd find something and I believed it; Emir was creative, intelligent, outgoing, and capable. The possibility that he might not find a way to stay did not cross my mind during those early conversations.

Emir talked with me about his visa situation because doing so was like asking a mechanic's daughter about engines. I grew up around visas because of my mother's job: Visa Chief. Chief of All Visas. Immigration Superhero Spy Extraordinaire. I learned so much from her during the years I tagged along. The immigration process was part of my early education. This made me the ideal friend with whom to discuss concerns about finding employer sponsorship for his H-1B work visa at the end of his OPT, the Optional Practical Training visa that followed the F-1 student visa.

The OPT allowed Emir to stay in the country and seek work in his field for one year following graduation. September 11th happened at the nine-month mark. Emir still hadn't found an employer willing to sponsor him. In the film industry, where entry-level positions were clerical and required no special skill, sponsorship was not worth the hassle of dealing with lawyers, documents, and filing fees. For a corporation, it was a bureaucratic annoyance. For a jobless Emir, December meant either deportation or trying to fly under the radar as an illegal immigrant. And this was before the attacks raised the stakes. Fewer jobs plus sudden suspicion of young men from Muslim countries meant finding sponsorship would be that much more difficult.

To be sponsored for a visa, a foreigner has to have an in-demand skill—a surgeon or engineer had far more of a chance than a young filmmaker, and after 9/11 even the best of the special skills set ran into visa troubles. One, for instance, was an infant cardiologist who developed groundbreaking procedures for operating on baby hearts. This man could not get back into the country because of bureaucratic red tape. So what chance did Emir stand?

In my living room, Emir sat on the beanbag chair that smelled vaguely of cat urine thanks to Sushi, the feral stray kitten the girls and I had taken in. I swiveled in the secondhand La-Z-Boy.

"Who will hire me after this?" he wondered aloud. "They'll take one look at my name on my resume and throw it in the garbage."

"People aren't that prejudiced," I repeated.

I wanted to believe it.

"If I go back I'll be enlisted in the mandatory military service. Can you imagine what they'll do to me in there?"

Emir had been trying for almost a year to find a means by which to stay, and September 11th marked the end of the expectation that anything would come from that trying. A feeling of anxiety permeated the air, the impact of the hijacked aircraft on the Twin Towers reverberating all the way to California, sinking us into a collective state of mourning. Who could focus on searching for clerical positions on Showbizdata.com when there were new images constantly flooding in of the attacks, the cleanup, the conspiracies? Going about our daily lives seemed self-indulgent.

It started long before this conversation, well before Emir's visa situation became an actual *problem*. It started out as more of a *concern* and spiraled down from there. When Emir first told me about it, I thought little, perhaps even nothing, of it, because of course it was going to work out. The universe would pull through, I believed. My outlook in my early twenties was that whatever was meant to happen would happen, that we have little capacity to exert control over the events in our lives. Believing that we were powerless to really change anything was an easy way to avoid responsibility. But something shifted when Emir talked to me about his visa. I tried to think of solutions for my friend, and then, suddenly, *what we ought to do about it* struck me with such a force that I knew I had hit on *the* answer, only it felt more as if it hit me, a bolt of lightning. For a brief moment, something made sense.

"I know!" I said. "I'll marry you!"

I couldn't save my father. I couldn't marry Julian. For Emir, I could do both. Save him by marrying him.

"Don't joke around with me about that, sweetie," he said.

But I already knew I wasn't kidding.


There were so many layers to the benefits. I'd been ready to marry and yet not really ready at all. Improvement at anything comes from practice and repetition, and this would be the only opportunity I would ever encounter to have a real live practice marriage. Why I didn't move in with Julian suddenly made a weird sort of sense: *Was this the bend in the road I could not see past? Was this the thing?* Yes! Yes of course, this was it! *I* could be the one to save my friend; I would assume the role of caretaker, protecting him from deportation and danger back in Emiristan. He offered companionship without the possibility of unbearable heartache. It was the ideal option for him, too, as the easiest way to get a green card is to marry a U.S. citizen, a rule that legally applied only to one man and one woman.

Larger issues and questions surrounded our circumstance, though they were not on my mind at the time: What makes a marriage? Why couldn't a gay person immigrate a same-sex partner? Why were immigration rights gender-biased? Immigration is a federal-level concern, and same-sex marriage is state law, so the federal government, at the time, did not recognize unions between gay citizens at all. In 1996, President Bill Clinton passed DOMA, the Defense of Marriage Act, into law. Finally struck down by the Supreme Court in 2013, DOMA defined marriage as "a legal union between one man and one woman as husband and wife." While shows like *The Bachelor, The Bachelorette, Who Wants to Marry a Millionaire?,* and *Married by America* were popular, President George W. Bush gave speeches about the sanctity of marriage and the need for a constitutional amendment defining marriage as between one man and one woman.

Heterosexuals can immigrate foreign spouses in a simple matter of signing a few forms—an American man can order a Russian or Chinese wife off the Internet—and members of same-sex couples couldn't immigrate the person they love simply because they share a gender. How can this qualify as anything other than discrimination? As if we even have a choice when it comes to whom we love, and I don't believe we do. This falling isn't a choice. It happens whether or not you want it, whether you're looking for an edge over which to leap or not. Most often, such falling happens when it's least expected.

Suddenly I felt a sense of purpose and direction that I'd never felt before, not about school, a career, or even engagement to Julian. I had never been this sure about anything. Marriage was perfect, fail-safe, and by far the best option. The very thing I'd been wanting—in a frantic mode that verged on desperation—to do in the first place. Why didn't I think of it before? *I was seeking asylum too!*

It felt like, well, fate—what I chose to believe in, because it meant everything was moving according to some divine plan (I was an atheist who held these ideas in my head simultaneously), and that in the end it would all somehow make sense. The other thing I knew marriage to Emir would give me, right off the bat, was an agenda, something to *do*. I had been drifting aimlessly in L.A., searching for meaning and not really finding it in the prop houses and paint shops my art department jobs brought me to. Marrying Emir to keep him with me would be an act that spoke to all of my beliefs about the world, the values my mother instilled: we live in a global village, we must love and respect and honor all cultures and all kinds of people. A Jewish-Italian-American straight girl and a gay boy from a Muslim family—we would transcend those "It's a Small World" Benetton ads and stand for something greater than ourselves. It seemed presented to me as a gift: marrying Emir would potentially save his life, and it also happened to merge the partnership I so craved with the doing of a good deed—a form of passive activism that brought to mind that 1980s perfume ad campaign: "make a statement without saying a word."

I was beginning to realize I had a complicated relationship with the act of marriage, and I was sure I wouldn't be entering into a marriage anytime in the foreseeable future. I didn't think anyone could take the place in my heart that Julian had occupied, so, I thought, I may as well use my ability and right to marry for a good reason. Then it would not go to waste. Yes, it made all kinds of sense, this spontaneous solution to both Emir's and my dilemmas. Definitions of family and marriage are ever evolving, anyway. It is said that families are the building blocks of society. Platonic: the word that described the nature of our relationship came from the philosopher who described the ideal society as one that removed partiality by abolishing family ties so that all citizens could care for one another equally. Aristotle argued against this notion, stating, "There are two things above all that make people love and care for something. The thought that it is all theirs, and the thought that it is the only one they have." Apparently the debate about what defined a family had been going on for eons. Who was to say Emir and I wouldn't "count" as a real one? He was already family to me.

People often assume the marriage proposal was Emir's idea and are surprised when I say it was mine. Though the proposal wasn't premeditated, I already knew how much I meant it. He needed the green card, and I needed him. I widened my eyes at him, smiling and waiting expectantly for what I was sure would be his wholehearted appreciation of my ingenious plan. But Emir looked at the floor.

"That's amazing and generous, but I can't. *We* can't."

"Why not?"

"What if we got caught?"

"For what?"

"For being in a fake marriage."

He said it as if he was explaining it to the kind of child who persisted every answer to a basic question with a resounding *BUT WHY?* I understood Emir's point, but I disagreed.

"What makes it fake, exactly?" I asked. "The last presidential election was based on a lie."

"What is this, Oral Rhetoric?"

At Emerson, which was originally a college of oratory, students were required to take Oral Rhetoric, a course in which we learned the art of crafting a convincing argument.

"Seriously though. There's so much dishonesty in the world, so much evil. We really care about each other, and marriage is so personal to the two people in it, anyway. So how do you judge a marriage entered into with *emotional authenticity* as false?"

"The INS would. It's all black-and-white to them."

"When couples find themselves in this situation, immigration officials ask if they love each other enough to get married, because marriage is the easiest, fastest, least complicated solution. Besides, I know the color of your toothbrush."

"What color is my toothbrush?"

"It's white and it's got a green stripe running down the middle."

He looked a little bit impressed.

"And no offense but you could stand to replace it. The bristles are all distorted. My mother says we should get those mechanical ones . . ."

"Sweetie, even if you know *every detail* of my toothbrush, I am still not willing to put you at risk. Tell me how I could live with myself if you were arrested or fined two hundred grand because of me, because you tried to help me?"

"I also know how you play Sims until five in the morning a lot of nights."

"All my friends know that."

"What's some weird little thing about me?"

"Your lips go white when you're nervous or scared."

"Really?"

He nodded. I had never looked in the mirror when I was nervous or scared. That was why it was easier for others to know in an instant what could take us years to know or understand about ourselves. We don't see our own expressions or feel what we radiate outward.

"Let's face it," I said. "We know each other about as well as any other couple that decides to get married. Probably even better than some. My parents knew each other for three months when they got married."

Emir buried his fingers in his curly dark hair and was silent, staring at the floor. His sneaker-clad foot tapped on the hard-wood. He seemed to be seriously considering. Then he looked up at me. His dark eyes locked with mine.

"What about your mother?" he asked.

"Yeah, there's that. But, I mean, so what?"

"*So what?* YOUR MOTHER IS AN IMMIGRATION PERSON. You don't see how this is perhaps a problem?"

"We don't have to tell her."

"But can't she find out with like the click of a button?"

"It's called the Consular Consolidated Database, but she has more important people to look up in there than you, no offense."

"You don't think this idea is too crazy?" He shook his head. I had argued my case, but had to admit he had a point. My mother worked to prevent immigration fraud and illegal immigration. "I'm a profiler, it's what I do for a living," she said when I accused her of judging people—pretty much always boyfriends of mine—too harshly. If she learned I married Emir for his green card, she would take it as a personal betrayal. I feared she might turn us in 1) to teach me a lesson, and 2) because it was her job. But my mother lived thousands of miles away while Emir and I made a point to meet for coffee, lunch, or drinks at least once a week. My mother wouldn't suffer if I married Emir, but Emir would suffer if I didn't. I would have an official new family member, one I could confide in, one who never judged.

My mother and I were a micro-family, just the two of us. She joined the Foreign Service in the early 1980s, after recruiters came through Seattle seeking female applicants. My mother decided to take the entrance exam on a whim, I was given an activity book about moving called *Goodbye House*, and we were off, from Seattle to D.C. for her training, and then to Guadalajara, Mexico in 1985. Some kids played house. I played home.

My father came to Guadalajara for the first year but my mother divorced him before the tour was over. I was six. My father, a Northern Italian immigrant from a family of farmers, moved back to Seattle with his green card and took back his old job at the fancy Italian restaurant where he waited tables. My mother and I kept moving, to Rome and eventually, Mexico

City. Thirteen years of Foreign Service life later, I left her to go to college. My mother—my family—lived six thousand nine hundred and eight miles away.

On fifth-grade winter break in Rome, 1989, my mother took me to see a movie called *New York Stories*. Of the series of vignettes, the part I remember was called "Oedipus Wrecks." Woody Allen plays a lawyer whose mother annoys him so much he wishes she would disappear. When a magic show trick goes wrong, Woody Allen's character gets his wish: the mother vanishes. But then she turns up again, and when she does, she's bigger than ever, larger than life: she looms in the sky over Manhattan, observing and commenting on her son's every move. Back outside on the street, when that frightening scene arose in conversation, my mother said, "That's me! If you're ever about to do something you shouldn't, remember me, The Big Mom in the Sky."

I was horrified. My mother smiled.

I didn't see what Emir took to calling "the mother thing" as an obstacle, but rather the uncanny coincidence that made me the perfect person to shepherd Emir through the immigration process, because I was, well, uniquely qualified. I knew more about immigration and visas than a person my age should have. As far as my mother was concerned, I wouldn't tell her—not only out of fear of what she had the power to do, but also to protect her. That way, there was not a chance of her career being affected by my choice, or of her being able to use my jeopardizing her career and professional reputation as a reason why I should not marry Emir.

Afternoon turned to evening and there was, as with many nights, a party. Jen and Kate came home and people trickled in, the random acquaintances we'd made over the course of our year in L.A. Someone took a picture of Emir and me. We hadn't moved from the spot: I sit on the secondhand La-Z-Boy and he is crouched beside me. In the photograph, our heads are pressed together and we're smiling at the camera, clutching each other's arms. We could pass for twins, or lovers. Did love, as with the Velveteen Rabbit, make it real?

I wasn't sure, but I did know I wanted to do it. If he returned to Emiristan, he would be forced back into the closet not for the two years we'd have to be married to ensure his green card, but for life. Emir and I were as well-matched as any couple that might choose marriage: aside from everything we had in common and having fun together even when doing something boring, we were both in our early twenties, desired to be in relationships, and faced the obstacle of not knowing what that meant or how to do it. We wanted to be loved, singled out by another as special and never to be abandoned. Here was the right thing at the right time—something manageable. If we have soul mates for different times in our lives, he would be mine for that era. My initial thought process went something like this: romantic love is difficult and complicated. Marrying your best friend to keep him with you, by comparison, is not.

Sometime before my parents divorced, I overheard my father say, "let's give Liza a little brother." My mother didn't want another child. She wanted out of the marriage. The possibility of the brother lingered with me long after my father left. Emir wasn't going anywhere. He offered constant companionship without the risk of heartbreak.

Our marriage would also serve as a litmus test for relationships. Any man who couldn't understand why marrying Emir was important to me was not open-minded enough for me. My world was porous, shape-shifting. Emir and I could depend on each other for unconditional filial love. This all added up to yet another situation that felt fated, the illusion that confirmed my life was taking a certain shape and direction in a time when it had none.

When I really thought about why I proposed to Emir—though the more I thought about it the more convinced I was that the reason was simply that I wanted to save my friend, that when he was around I was happier, that these two were reason enough—I still felt there was more to it than that. I wanted to pinpoint my motivation because I am a stickler for reasons, for understanding what drives a person, even when it may be impossible to determine.

Why do we get married? Desire, what we learn from our parents—because we want a teammate for the competitive sport of modern capitalist life, someone to journey with, that whole us-against-the-world thing? Plain old tradition, because it's simply "what people do"? Better benefits? In my case, with Emir, there was also the question of compassion.

I was two months away from my twenty-second birthday, living in L.A. after breaking off my engagement to the man I'd thought I would marry since I was sixteen, striving for a career in *entertainment*. I drove around all day photographing objects, skimming the surface of surfaces. Swimming in these shallow waters, my entire existence felt like one giant exercise in self-serving narrowness. Here was one thing that did not. But was it compassion for Emir, or was this, too, a selfish act? Is compassion fundamentally selfish, something we can employ to feel good about ourselves when we are such flawed creatures?

I can say it was my international, uprooted childhood that allowed me the initial mindset to propose to Emir. I can say it was subconscious rebellion against my mother. I can say it was deception, a mirroring of circumstances, a family tradition. I can say it was solidarity. I can give all kinds of reasons but the truth was a combination of them all and yet none of them as a whole.

I fixated on reasons, but how much do reasons matter? There was the simple surface: that he was a friend in need and I could help. But there are deeper levels to what drives us during the more extreme situations we encounter, levels to which we are guaranteed neither access nor understanding.

After the initial shock of the terrorist attacks died down, everyone got busy revisiting their priorities. For Jen and Kate, this entailed moving back to Boston. We had been reminded of our mortality, that safety was an illusion and our lives could end at any instant, while trapped in a burning plane or sitting at our desks at work. California wasn't the paradise they expected to find. Jen went back to Emerson, Kate to photography school. They moved on, replacing themselves in our West Hollywood apartment with another female roommate we knew from college. With Jen and Kate gone, Emir was my only friend in

L.A. We both had mixed feelings about our latest home. Emir called it "desert culture." Everyone in their cars, shielded from the elements, nomadically passing by. The opportunities in our industry were here but the city itself was isolating. We missed certain things about the East Coast, walking and what Jack Kerouac called "a feeling of wacky comradeship somewhere in some streets." L.A. never felt quite like home, but Emir and I were used to this, too. Emir grew up in one native country with a culture that would reject him if he came out as a young gay man, and I moved around every few years to foreign countries where—as visitor, as guest—I, too, learned to blend in.

While I was feeling valiant about the marriage possibility, Emir remained skeptical. *We* were one man and one woman, I reminded him over dinner, at the dry cleaner's, in line at the gay Starbucks. Maybe he would say yes just to get me to stop bugging him.

Emir made a good point, though. *Would* it be real? If love was the driving force behind a proposal, who but the two people in the marriage could say whether that love was substantial enough to be legal? The aporia was overwhelming. Seeking answers, I dove into research. I came across an article about an Orthodox Jewish lesbian and gay man marrying and adopting children, choosing to live a celibate life as a family rather than any alternative because of their religious beliefs. I read that it isn't illegal to marry someone for tax purposes, or because you both have red hair, or love attending Star Trek conventions in your spare time. You can get married for any reason you please.

Emir was adamant in his refusal every time I brought it up, citing my safety as the reason. He was concerned about putting me at risk, while I was determined to assume any, whatever it took. My offer to marry Emir transcended his visa needs. My reason for wanting to keep him in the country was fundamentally selfish: it guaranteed the existence of one person who couldn't leave me. Who hasn't wanted to keep someone he or she loves from going away, from leaving? It wasn't a choice I grappled with. I cared about Emir enough that if a government bureaucrat in a fluorescent-lit office challenged us, I would fight for our status as "real."

At the time, I would have stood firm in that I was selflessly offering my hand in help, but as my friend Emily, a psychoanalyst's daughter, later wrote, "altruism is a form of escape from one's own unconscious anger and desires." (We learn so much from our mothers!) She was talking about herself—she had a job working with refugees—but it occurred to me that our predicaments were more similar than I realized. And I thought about "The Junky's Christmas," the high that came from helping another human being. It suddenly seemed a most auspicious beginning for Emir and me.

## 3.

## Two Brides a-Blushing, No Golden Rings . . .

The stories dominating the headlines made me increasingly concerned for, and obsessed with, Emir and his safety. Tarek Mohamed Fayad, an Egyptian dental student, had been arrested at gunpoint in nearby San Bernardino. Fayad had taken fewer than twelve credit hours one semester when he was sick, which violated the terms of his student visa. He was sent back to Egypt. He was one of many. Since the usual immigration channels were dammed, several best-case scenarios involved the euphemistic "voluntary departure."

The news grew more frightening. In Arizona, gas station owner Balbir Singh Sodhi was shot to death. He wasn't Muslim or Middle Eastern, but a Sikh. Sodhi was Punjabi, and in the late 1980s he immigrated to Los Angeles, where he worked as a taxi driver. He did the same in San Francisco. He drove taxis until he saved enough to buy a gas station. His own business. The American Dream. The murderer operated under the false principle that Sodhi was Muslim because he wore a turban, unaware that Muslims don't wear turbans.

Voices on talk radio spoke of terrorism and border security, and about plans for young males from Middle Eastern nations: interviews, fingerprinting, photographs, questionnaires. Even those already in the country with green cards and work visas could be retroactively screened, while those awaiting green cards and visas faced months of delays. Breaches in procedure, no matter how minor, could result in being banned from the United States for five years, sometimes more. The term "bureaucratic nightmare" was redefined overnight.

Emir tried everything else: more job applications, the green card lottery—he entered every year since he moved to Boston at eighteen, and every year heard nothing—asylum, and graduate school. To go back to school he would have to leave the country to wait for a new student visa before he could return. The odds were not in his favor. The new security reviews in place caused months of delays. The smallest mistakes could lead to deportation.

I told Emir that the marriage offer was still on the table if all else failed.

A miracle could still happen—a job, a green card lottery win. . . . Either way, Emir would not consent to a marriage arrangement. Unlike me, he did not believe that the we-love-each-other justification would work with the authorities if they suspected he was gay. He kept turning it around on me: he didn't want to put me in danger, he didn't want anything bad to happen to me, he didn't want to be the reason for a permanent rift between my mother and me.

He pointed out some of the flaws in my plan: I would marry him to stop him from going back to his father's house to live a double life, but he would instead be living a double life in the States for the minimum of two years it took for the green card to become permanent. I would marry him so he would not end up in an arranged marriage with a woman, but that was exactly what he'd be getting into. He would have to go back into the closet for the wedding and INS interviews.

I asked my mother for advice on his behalf, without mentioning my "fallback plan." She was used to my badgering her about types of visas, visiting artist or exceptional talent ones, and whether someone's asylum case was likely to be approved, so asking would not raise suspicion that I was ready to solve Emir's problem myself. I asked my mother questions on behalf of foreign friends all the time. Her response was not unusual either, and nothing Emir didn't already know: he needed to find a job. An employer petitioning for an H-1B work visa was the only option other than seeking asylum.

Seeking asylum was a long and complicated process that likely wouldn't go through in the end. Emir's friend Omar, a man he met through his West Hollywood network, sought asylum, got denied, and was tied up in an endless process of appeals. Omar attended law school and wanted to specialize in immigration reform, especially after his failed asylum bid.

Immigration judges reject asylum on the grounds that petitioners' lives do not appear to be at risk. Applicants have been rejected, sent home, and killed by the very thing they were escaping, whether Salvadoran street gangs or Middle Eastern gay-bashers. Some applicants in Emir's situation have been rejected for not being "gay enough."*

"There's really nothing that's more of a sure bet?" I asked.

"It's very difficult," my mother said. "American workers have priority for American jobs. I had a person in here yesterday asking about going to live in the U.S., but you can't just go live there . . . it has to be job- or school-related or you need to have an immediate family member immigrate you. Can't he try Canada? Their immigration policy offers more . . . possibilities."

"Okay, thanks. I'll let him know about Canada."

Canada. Yeah, right. Emir wasn't moving to Canada. Nothing against Canada but the whole point was to keep him in West Hollywood.

Though my mother worked in consulates, I privately wondered if perhaps she was a spy. She pointed out spies to me at diplomatic parties; they were the most unassuming people in the room, more Star Trek convention–attendee than James Bond. Was my mother among them? I imagined her obtaining classified information for the government with the charm she could turn on and off as by a switch. People called her "vivacious." She elicited this adjective above all others and I heard it over and over at these functions because it was true.

She went to a lot of fancy diplomatic parties where people stood around talking about international affairs. Her vivaciousness meant people opened up to her easily. She was just a warm mom. Look, she even brought her little daughter—the

---

*   www.nytimes.com/2011/01/29/nyregion/29asylum.html

quiet one sitting in the corner over there, eating all the hors d'oeuvres—isn't she sweet?

The immigrant smuggler and the spy, each keeping secrets from the other: we were the premise for a surrealist Aesop fable. My mother had unintentionally raised me to be the type of person to see marrying Emir as a rational act, a reasonable solution. Though it seemed contradictory to what she did for a living—screening people, making decisions about their likelihood of staying in the U.S. and working illegally on a tourist visa—she wanted this career in the first place for the opportunity to travel the world. When I was a teenager, we often had dinner table conversation about immigration cases and visas. Sometimes there was an interesting story from her day at the office. Other times, she complained about work.

"I have to deal with all these crazy Americans who go off their medication and wander down here," she said one evening when we lived in Mexico City. "Anyone can get on a bus. Then they show up in my office needing their families to wire money so they can get home."

I ate my pasta quietly, nodded, and listened.

"It's weird how any American can hop a bus to Mexico but the opposite could never happen."

I was sixteen and working in her office. Most Mexican applicants for tourist visas were rejected. I saw it on a daily basis.

"Lize," she said. "That's why I want you to realize how privileged we are to be able to carry these passports. We can go almost everywhere. A U.S. passport gives you freedom to see the world, freedom most people don't have."

"You're right, but it seems unfair."

"It is unfair. The borders should be more open. But it's still important to realize we're lucky."

She indoctrinated me into the "privileged homeless," preaching the value of internationalism, of making friends across all cultures and borders and viewing the world as a global village. But my mother didn't teach me to break the law, if that was indeed what Emir and I would be doing. If she found out, would she turn us in to teach us a lesson about illegal green card marriage? Could she do that, knowing Emir's life was at stake, and knowing how much I loved him? Because it was her job? Because she would feel betrayed not only as a consular officer but as a mother? I didn't want to find out, so I knew I would never tell her. It would be easier to keep it a secret, to hide in plain sight. After all, she had no reason to type Emir's name into the Consular Consolidated Database. Why would it ever occur to her to do that? She was so busy at work in the wake of September 11th, why would Emir's visa status cross her mind at all? I was sure we would be safe and that everything was going to be fine.

Only it wasn't fine.

As the visa was coming to an end, a deportation letter arrived.

On Halloween night, Emir and I were at the Abbey. He was Harry Potter and I was a cat. Emir was the spitting image of the magical boy in his round glasses and wizard-school uniform. Many of our West Hollywood friends, mostly foreign gay men, milled about the courtyard talking, flirting, and dancing. I was more comfortable here than anywhere, but that night Emir was preoccupied, tossing back dirty martinis until he was drunk. It had been another fruitless week of job hunting. It was about to be November, which meant his visa expired in a month. I took a gulp of my cocktail, hopped off the barstool, and got down on one knee.

"Lose an earring?" he asked.

"Will you please agree to be my blushing bride already?"

He hopped off his barstool, knelt beside me, and took my hands. I already knew that this time, this proposal, would be the one he accepted. The finality was palpable—this was not three months or two months but *one*. The countdown was nearing its end, and it was coming to the point where Emir's decision would boil down to accepting my offer, going illegal, or packing his bags for a return to Emiristan.

The choice was obvious.

"It would be an honor to be the envy of straight men everywhere," he said.

I laughed and scanned the patio. "Straight men? Where?"

Onlookers stared. It wasn't every day they witnessed a marriage proposal at The Abbey. I'd forgotten we were wearing costumes. Emir thanked me and I told him he didn't ever have to thank me. He was doing me a favor, too, even though he didn't know it, at least not overtly. I wouldn't have been able to articulate it then, but I was looking for a person who would not leave me. This wasn't exactly what I had in mind but it was a guarantee in a time when not even the ground felt solid. Emir and I would have to live together for at least the next two years, keep meticulous records showing we had a joint bank account, billing address, and tax returns. We would also have to take a lot of photographs.

"We can't tell anyone except our closest friends," Emir said. "We can't risk getting caught."

"Still with the 'getting caught?' Who's to say we don't 'count' as 'legitimate'? Why should I have to keep the nature of the most important relationship in my life a secret?"

Emir shrugged. "That's how gay people feel all the time," he said.

And so I was twenty-one and had been engaged twice—this time for the serious business of possibly duping the government to procure a green card. Most of my friends were still in college. How young I was did not occur to me then, so eager was I to settle down. And yet, although Emir and I would be married, we would continue being "single." We would both continue to sleep with men. We would have to be discreet about my dating and Emir's relationship with Adrian, as well as discreet about the marriage. We weren't going to give up sex—it was an open marriage—we just wouldn't be having it with each other. Emir would be with Adrian. I would try to get back out there and meet someone age-appropriate and compatible. But most importantly, Emir was not a stranger who was paying me, which would definitely constitute an illegal green card arrangement. He was my closest friend. That no compensation would be requested or received would be our legal shield—we hoped. This marriage was a gift, a promise to have each other's backs, to not up and leave and let our connection dissolve as so many of our friendships had during our transient youths.

Emir and I wouldn't have the issues that conventional couples did, but we'd been burned by those conventions anyhow. Ours would be a white marriage in many shades of gray.

Since, when it came to me, Emir cared about everything *except* sex, there were no questions, no games, and no sexual tension. He made me laugh, and made even the darkest stories funny. He was like me in that we both sought out the humor in pain. We were learning to laugh at ourselves, which became useful after my engagement to Julian ended, when I was prone to moping around, wallowing in the pathetic abyss known as self-pity. One such day in that time, I told Emir I wanted to come over and swim in his pool. "No one swims in that pool, sweetie. It's cold and full of leaves." Stubborn and determined, I jumped in anyway. My visions of closing my eyes and imagining I was poolside at the Beverly Hills Hotel were shattered as the freezing water numbed my skin. I emerged with dried leaves in my hair and goose bumps, dripping on the concrete.

"Enjoy your swim?" Emir asked, smiling from the patio.

So sometimes you want something to be other than what it is so badly you ignore the obvious. That engagement? A boyfriend and a ring do not a fiancé make. I wasn't ready and neither was Julian. As I thought about it, I became suspicious: Julian needed a green card, too. Had that motivated his proposal? The investment bank sponsored his H-1B, the work visa Emir had desperately sought all over Hollywood, but this meant Julian was anchored to the bank. He could not quit his job to look for another while keeping his visa, and he often complained that there were higher salaries to be found if only he were free to look. His ambition could not be measured, it was vast enough to swallow anything that dared step into its path. But I can't truly know his motives. How can we know another's when we can't even be entirely sure we understand our own?

Emir and I picked a date: November 17th, 2001, five days after my twenty-second birthday. What kind of wedding would we have? Something traditional that would be sure not to raise any eyebrows, or something more colorful and strange as an emblem of our unlikely merging? We sat side by side in his desk chair making our very first decision as a twosome.

"I don't want to wear a dress that looks like a float from the Macy's parade."

"We could find a nice little church somewhere . . ."

"Church?"

Neither of us had been to church but we knew the rundown from the romantic comedies we watched with tissues and low-fat popcorn.

"How about Vegas?" Emir proposed.

"What's more American, God or Elvis?"

The hardest part was choosing the location. There are over a hundred wedding chapels in Las Vegas. They bear names like "A Special Memory," "Graceland," "Cupid's," "Hollywood," and "Tuscany," all of which popped up when Emir typed "wedding,"

"Las Vegas," and "Elvis" into a search engine. We agreed on an Elvis package at the Viva Las Vegas Wedding Chapel, which offered other themed options including "Liberace," "Intergalactic," "Godfather," and "Starlet" ("Blonde Goddess Impersonator to perform ceremony and sing").

Emir told his father that our marriage was for the green card alone. He didn't want his father to think there was a chance we would fall in love during the course of this process; even though Emir wasn't out and had no plans at that point to come out to his father, he still didn't want to give false hope.

Mohammad wanted a grandson. Emir was the eldest and only son, heir to the company his father founded—which Emir wanted nothing to do with. His father had false hope regardless of what Emir told him. Mohammad knew enough couples in arranged marriages that he expected love would follow eventually. Familiarity did not breed contempt; rather, it grew into fondness. He would have preferred a Muslim girl but he was pleased enough with me to offer to pay for the wedding, which made us wonder if on some unconscious level Mohammad already knew.

Mohammad lied to his own mother about the marriage, spiraling out our circle of deception even further, telling her I was a Muslim girl Emir had met in the college's Islamic society. Our school didn't have an Islamic society. If she found out I was not Muslim, Granny would be livid. She'd also demanded that Emir bring me back right away so that she could approve this American bride.

"She would do things like tell you to get her a glass of water," Emir said, rolling his eyes. "The test would serve two purposes: she would be evaluating how you treat her as an elder, to gauge the amount of respect you show. And she would be checking out your ass."

"Why would your Granny be checking out my ass?"

"Because according to the old wives' tale, the bigger it is, the more likely you will have a boy."

"Ah, yes. Sons."

Only Emir's mother, Yalda, knew that the much-desired grandsons stood no chance of arriving via my womb . . . ever.

Emir and I threw our "engaygement" party at the Abbey. I wanted the invitations to say "Putting the Gay in Engagement Since 2001," but that was not exactly something we could paste into our INS album.

My only bridesmaid cancelled at the last minute. She wouldn't be attending the engaygement *or* the wedding. Her older sister, it turned out, told her she was getting involved with "an illegal green card arrangement." That she could be implicated—maybe even arrested as an accessory.

"When I told you I'd be in your wedding, I didn't know you were doing something illegal," she said as I protested.

I tried to push it out of my mind and enjoy the party.

The engaygement guests ultimately consisted of members of Emir's circle, the one I was marrying into: the boys of West Hollywood. They understood. I'd always felt a kinship with gay men, not that I expected them to provide me with entertainment or solace, and not that I loved every gay man I ever met, but for the most part, I felt especially alive in the company of my gay male friends. In the back cabana-lined grotto of the Abbey, Emir and I reclined on one of the beds, the royal couple for a night, as a few of his West Hollywood friends bought us glasses of champagne and toasted our impending union.

Emir introduced me to Omar, the man who was denied asylum. Omar, a self-described flaming queen who wore eyeliner and had liposuction to further tighten his already-firm stomach, was going to serve as the witness at our wedding.

"Where are you from?" I asked.

"I'm a quarter Lebanese, a quarter Iranian, a quarter French, a quarter Turkish, a quarter Canadian, and a quarter Dutch, a quarter Italian, and a quarter Pakistani."

He turned and walked away.

"That's a lot of quarters," I said to Emir.

"He's schizophrenic," Emir joked. "He has two personalities."

"And so therefore—"

"Eight quarters," we said at the same time.

Most of Emir's friends were expats. Besides the human United Nations that was Omar, in attendance were Emir's roommate, Said; Ali, a Lebanese real estate agent; Jenk, who was Turkish; and Jean-Claude, Frenchman. And Adrian, Emir's boyfriend. I still didn't know him very well. Maybe I enjoyed thinking I was the most important person in Emir's life. I had a tendency to envy other people who shared his love, even though I knew this was absurd; Emir had to have a life, a fulfilling life, outside of "us," just as I did, as any two people in a close relationship should. As I saw the other Em come into the party, though, in a sparkling silver sequined minidress, a cascade of blonde curls tumbling down her back, the jealousy surged again. Boyfriends were one thing. Another girlfriend was a different matter entirely. I watched her cross the patio, watched her kiss Emir once on each cheek, and wished her next movie would send her on location to Timbuktu.

Em was Emma, Emir's other girlfriend. They'd met while out and about in the neighborhood. She was a tall, blonde actress married to a scientist who was off on a submarine under the sea somewhere. I guessed that both these reasons—being unbearably gorgeous and having an absentee husband—were the reasons she frequented gay bars. When I'd gone to dinner with their group in the past, I heard people referring to them as Em & Em, Meer and Ma, and Em-girl and Em-boy. I felt guilty about the jealousy, said nothing, and pretended it was no big deal. Emir had a right to other close female friends . . . though I didn't want any of those friendships with other girls to be as close as ours. I wanted to be his best girl.

As the wedding date approached, I gave more thought to the arguments that what we were doing was illegal. The types of arguments my mother would make if she knew. This was immigration fraud. Emir and I were not "in love" in the way that's expected of married couples in Western society. No sex or romance was involved. If it's unconsummated, it's illegal, end of story. We danced a blurry legal line. People have been arrested for green card marriages, but no one like us—not a close pair who lived together and shared their lives as we did. It seemed like a big gray area to me. What if, after Emir and I became successful screenwriters with a Hollywood Hills villa, we adopted an entourage of international, multiethnic children and lived as progressive-minded citizens of the world? What negative consequences, other than annoying our old college friends, could there be?

Marriage did not guarantee a lifelong tie. I knew as much from my parents and the divorce rate. People entered marriages that they knew, whether by gut feeling or concretely, weren't going to be for life. People married for money. For tax breaks. Infertile couples could marry, so procreation wasn't the issue. What, then, defined us as unqualified? After the no-fault divorce was introduced into American society in the 1950s, marriage was no longer as binding a tie as it had been in the past. It could be argued our marriage was illegitimate given we "knew" that it would eventually end, but entering a marriage with doubts of its "foreverness" was not illegal. Marriages and friendships do end, children get emancipated, sole custody is granted. Change is the only constant. Everything ends eventually. But did we know this at the outset? We didn't know anything of what was to come. What if we decided to stay married for life? If emotional fulfillment could come from one place, sexual gratification from another, it could happen. Or, as with my desire to be a rooted epiphyte, would it prove an impossible contradiction? I loved blurring lines, playing with definitions, and pushing boundaries. This marriage that was more like an adoption of sorts wasn't just about a green card—it was an experiment in consciousness, a provocation, an exercise.

Are feelings ever factual? Ultimately, I couldn't say whether it was real or not—that is not for me to decide or a question for this story to answer—but I had no desire to talk to lawyers, engage argument, hear the word "no." I knew what advice I would have gotten and I didn't want it. It would have felt so Romeo and Juliet: he is of the Gays! And you, the Straights! And never the twain shall marry!

*Please,* I responded to my imaginary challenger. *Movie stars do this all the time.*

As George W. Bush said, "The union of *a man and a woman* is the most enduring human institution, honored and encouraged in all cultures and by every religious faith." A man and a woman—that was us!

The Defense of Marriage Act defined it so.

And better to be a second-class citizen in America than gay in Emiristan.

I would be far from the first to marry a man to keep him in the country, and not only in terms of a green card. In 1965, a presidential order was issued stating that men married after August 26th of that year would be on the same order of draft call as single men. A 1963 order had placed married men lower on the list. One hundred and seventy-one couples were married in Las Vegas the night before the new order went into effect.

In "Marrying Absurd," Joan Didion notes that one justice of the peace married sixty-seven of those couples. I failed to see much difference between marrying to improve someone's draft status and marrying to keep someone in the country. Both were overriding the system because one person did not want to lose another by the government's orders. Man versus machine.

# 4.

## Visa Las Vegas

"Yes, I am mindful that we're all sinners. And I caution those who may try to take the speck out of the neighbor's eye when they've got a log in their own."                                                —George W. Bush

The next time I looked up, the open road was gone. Casinos, strip clubs, and a billboard of two four-story men embracing a three-story white tiger came into view, signs of entering Las Vegas, City of Sin. The high noon sun glared overhead, casting white-hot light over Circus Circus, the Bellagio, and Versace and Prada storefronts. As Emir and I cruised by in his rusty blue '92 Nissan Sentra, it was as though we had come upon a colonized patch of an otherwise dark, distant planet. I both loved and loathed Las Vegas, that beacon of excess and illusion, its bath of neon lights tainting the expansive desert.

The ride had been monotonous—flat, colorless land and tract housing. Emir gave me his laptop and insisted I watch a show he loved called *Sex and the City*. It was at the height of its popularity, but I didn't have a television and had not seen it. Emir tried to get me to watch certain shows on a regular basis. Usually I refused, he wore me down, and then I watched whatever he was suggesting and found myself hooked. *Sex and the City* was no different. Carrie's puns about crossing the line between professional girlfriend and "just plain professional" reminded me that I was about to become a professional wife. Though not exactly. It would be more of an unpaid internship.

Wedding weekend would be Emir's first time in Vegas. I'd been there twice before during the year in L.A., quick road trips with Jen and Kate—twelve hours and back by dawn. If I stayed any longer, I became consumed by feelings of anxiety and doom, that the ground beneath the fake Luxor pyramid might open up and swallow me whole into a labyrinthine tomb where I would be mummified in a paste of lost hundred-dollar bills.

I didn't tell Emir that three days earlier, my mother had been the star of a different kind of ceremony, as the recipient of an award from the INS for her work preventing illegal immigration, the timing so ridiculous it felt as if the universe were giving me a poke in the ribs. Emir exited the Vegas Strip at West Tropicana Avenue and we checked into Motel 6, the largest one in the country. Emir chose it. Mohammad was footing the bill for our wedding weekend but we still didn't want anything fancy and expensive. Hotel rooms were for sleeping and we wouldn't be doing much of that.

I didn't tell my mother that I was going to Las Vegas. Since I'd gotten a cell phone, it was easy to say I was home or running some errands or something routine. My mother and I would have our usual weekend phone call. I would congratulate her on the award and she would have no idea that I was in Las Vegas taking care of an immigration case of my own.

Emir and I toured the Strip all afternoon. It almost felt like an ordinary holiday. We traveled well together—a benchmark of a good relationship. That day, we realized both of us referred to the hotel as home, as in "let's go home and get ready." Recognizing that shared detail, we smiled at each other; as with many instances between us, there was no need for words.

The speed of Las Vegas can also mean you find yourself alone in a motel bathroom at nightfall with the wrong part of you feeling light—not your heart but your head. Suddenly, it all felt as if it was happening too fast, as if despite my careful thinking I hadn't thought it through enough. The reality of what Emir and I were about to do—about to *become*—began to set in. I was no longer sure whether this would be the perfect starter marriage or an exercise in despair. I picked up eyeliner from the edge of the sink and leaned in close to the mirror, attempting to draw a straight black line and failing. My hand shook. There was a light rapping at the door.

"Need help in there?" Emir called from the other side.

On a typical night I would have sat on the toilet lid as Emir applied my eyeliner, but, as I had repeated for many years at my grandmother's Seder table, this night was different.

"You're not supposed to see the bride before she's ready!" I shouted, not wanting him to witness my tentative state.

I had to pull it together but I couldn't stop thinking about my mother and how disappointed she would be if she knew what I was doing, and not only because it was a secret wedding to Emir but also because it was a huge secret I was keeping from her. I knew she imagined being there for her daughter's wedding, and how happy she was when I'd gotten engaged to Julian. Besides her view that this was an illegal green card marriage, that Emir and I were about to defraud the U.S. Government and debase and defile everything she worked so hard for in her twenty-five-year career, she would also be hurt not to have been invited to her only child's wedding. By helping Emir I was still rebelling against her. My mother prevented immigration violations and I was going to be the most badass immigration violator ever.

I emerged from the bathroom and there was Emir, looking snazzy in his belted khakis, bright red shirt, shiny burgundy tie, and dark brown leather jacket. Suddenly I worried that my hot pink paisley halter shift was hideous.

"Love the dress," he said when he saw me.

Omar waited in the lobby. Not your classic matrimonial sojourner, he was perfect for our circus sideshow of a ceremony, his shiny button-down shirt tucked into tight leather pants and eyebrows plucked into flawless arches. His eyeliner, unlike my own, was perfectly applied.

"Happy wedding night!" Omar said, beaming as if he were a proud parent.

Then he went to the front desk to call us a taxi. The sliding glass doors slid open as Emir and I stepped outside into the warm Vegas night. Emir lit a cigarette. We stood there in our unconventional wedding outfits. He smoked and we looked at each other.

"Are you nervous?" I asked.

"Are you?" He tested the waters.

"Yeah."

"Oh, good. I was feeling bad about being so nervous."

"In the bathroom, I thought I was going to throw up."

We laughed.

"Why are we so nervous?" I asked.

"We're getting married! No matter what, that is a big deal. And do either of us really want to do this? I love you, but do you think this is something I would do for fun?"

Omar came outside.

"Who gets married for *fun*?" He chimed in. "Marriage isn't fun!"

Our taxi pulled up.

"It can be," I said. "This one will."

We got in and the driver sped toward the Viva Las Vegas wedding chapel.

"Why aren't any of *your* friends here?" Omar asked me.

"They moved back to Boston. And the friend I asked to be my bridesmaid backed out because her sister convinced her this was illegal and that if she joined us she could be implicated."

Even friends didn't make the distinction between Emir and I getting married and the green card marriages depicted in Hollywood—movies like *Green Card* and, later, *The Proposal*. The couples in these movies always fall in love in the end. It's practically a plot requirement.

"Then let's stop for some champagne, yes?" Omar said. "Your nerves are obviously in need of calming."

Omar sprang for a bottle of Veuve Clicquot and we drank it out of a paper bag in the taxi. The bottle was empty by the time we arrived at the chapel. From the outside, the chapel resembled a chain restaurant, the Olive Garden of matrimonial structures.

"They're ready for you," the blue-eyed receptionist told us. "Just give me your marriage license and we'll get going."

"The what?" Emir asked.

"The marriage license?" she repeated.

*Oh no.*

Emir and I were so young and naïve we didn't realize you had to get a marriage license in order to get married. We thought all we had to do was show up at the chapel. It was Elvis! Who thought about paperwork? Apparently, everyone but us.

"Is there still time to go to the wherever and get it?" Emir asked the receptionist.

"Minister Frank?" she squawked into an intercom. "Can you come out here, please? Bit of a problem with these next ones."

A gentle-seeming older man with thinning white hair emerged from the chapel. He wore jeans tucked into cowboy boots.

"What seems to be the matter? Commitment jitters? We offer premarital counseling for a small additional fee—"

"They forgot the license," the receptionist said.

"Uh-oh." The minister glanced at his watch.

"Is there any way Elvis can wait?" Emir asked. "We'll run and get it . . ."

"Gonna be crowded down there on a Saturday night."

"Please," I said.

"I can pay for an extra time slot or something," said Emir.

"We can switch the order of the evening," the receptionist chimed in. "Put the Mafia wedding ahead of them. That party is already here."

"Then tell Joe to hold off on getting dressed," the minister said.

Emir asked where we had to go and the receptionist told us to get in any taxi and tell them we were going to the marriage license office. It was open twenty-four hours then. I was not surprised that neither of us understood how to go about getting married.

We ran out of the chapel and hailed another taxi. The night air in the desert gave me chills. Omar jumped into the front seat, Emir and I in back.

"Marriage license place, please," Omar said.

The driver, a tattooed Las Vegas version of Santa Claus, turned to face Emir and me.

"You kids forgot a license before your wedding?" he asked. He shook his head and slammed on the gas. Tires squealed as we flew out of the parking lot and back out onto the boulevard. The driver's eyes were on us in the rearview mirror.

"Relax, son," he said to Emir. "Not the first time it's happened."

"I think we had too much champagne," I said, imagining the driver as a deranged substitute dad. Maybe he could walk me down the aisle. Then I noticed the tears in Emir's eyes. I rubbed his shoulders.

"It's okay, sweetie, we got this."

"You guys," said Omar, "both of you, calm down. We will go there, procure the license, and all will be well."

I never thought I would feel so grateful for the presence of a man in eyeliner.

"And you are fabulous," he continued, looking me over head to toe. "I mean, in that dress, honey, no one would ever know you didn't have a totally flat stomach."

Well, maybe not *that* grateful.

We asked the taxi driver to wait as we rushed out toward the door of the marriage license office. We stood in line under the fluorescent lights. A sense of reality sunk in, one that is conspicuously absent when one is hanging around with costumed Elvises and people who book Mafia-themed weddings. It occurred to me that marriage is an interesting and contradictory mix of romance and bureaucracy.

My eyes wandered around the room, curious about who else was getting marriage licenses at this hour. The other couples were a blonde lady with a Mexican man in a Dodgers cap; a goth couple who didn't look a day older than eighteen; a dowdy pregnant brunette with a man missing a front tooth; an excited Asian couple chattering in Japanese and snapping photos; and a short, muscular, olive-skinned man with a cute, petite, brown-haired girl. I wondered which of these other couples were marrying for green card purposes and which held the Las Vegas wedding as a lifelong dream. Were any of them eloping to avoid over-involved relatives? Who met at the craps tables earlier tonight? I wondered if any of them would get an annulment in the morning. I overheard a bride-to-be say, "It's like we're just running errands. It doesn't feel like we're getting married."

I could relate. I was still operating under the assumption that marriage with Emir would be conflict-free, seamless, and simple because Emir was gay. Getting married, especially in Las Vegas, may be easy, but I had no idea what would come next—which, even in a sexless marriage, could be messier and more complicated than I ever would have imagined. This was our fun night. Our respite before there was anything to desire a respite from. I thought about my mother walking down an aisle of her own to accept that award for her work preventing illegal immigration.

"Can we go first?" Emir asked the couple who were about to see the license-granter. He quickly explained what had happened. The woman, the pregnant brunette, said absolutely, please, go ahead. We stepped in front of them—next to be called, maybe we would make good time after all. The man gave us a steely look and muttered something under his whiskey-soaked breath that sounded like "sand monkeys." I'd never heard the phrase before. When I later looked it up online I was livid.

After signing the paperwork, Emir paid the fifty-five-dollar fee and the license was ours.

A pause in the doorway for a quick photo, and it was chapel time for real. We ran back out onto the street and into our waiting taxi. The driver smiled in the rearview mirror and shook his head.

We caught the end of the gangster ceremony. A couple who resembled figures out of a Botero painting said their vows to an elderly actor dressed in a Mafioso suit. I gawked at the unreality of it all. Emir squeezed my hand. *The Godfather* theme music cranked up as these smiling and rosy-faced people entered the you-may-kiss portion of the vows. I was most nervous about this—having to kiss Emir on the lips. Even if I tried to as a sort of mind game with myself, I couldn't see Emir in a sexual way, though we talked about sex all the time. The prospect of this kiss was vaguely nauseating, and not because Emir is unattractive. Quite the opposite. Men approached him all the time when we were out together in West Hollywood. I just didn't see him that way. I loved Emir the way I imagined I would love my brother, if I had a brother. And now, in a sense, I would. This was one of the primary reasons I could marry Emir. Our arrangement wouldn't be complicated by sex. The gangster couple leaned in. They looked happy. I wondered what I was.

"I'm in love, I'm all shook up," our fake Elvis sang.

This was our cue.

# 5.
# Hound Dogs and
# Blue Suede Shoes

"Marriage is also, like love, a many-splendored thing, its splendor having sacred, social, and political dimensions."
—Mark Carl Rom

Plastic trees and fabric foliage behind the Elvis impersonator shuddered with the reverb. There was no father to walk me down the aisle but this was the perfect distraction from that fact. Emir and I danced down it, shaking our hips, spinning and twirling in sync like whirling dervishes. The whole environment made it easy to forget. I felt as if we were acting in a high school musical. The Elvis impersonator spun around. His black hair was slicked up with grease. His costume consisted of oversized sunglasses and a shiny red silk button-down rhinestone-studded jumpsuit.

"Seriously?" I whispered to Emir.

"Shhhh . . ." he attempted to hush me, but the absurdity of the situation as much as Elvis's getup and hip gyrations made us both laugh anyway. Omar clapped on the sidelines, snapping pictures all the while for our INS album. It was the most fun I'd had since the end of my first engagement.

"The minister is gay," Emir said into my ear. "And I think he might know."

"Act straighter," I murmured back as we made our way toward Elvis.

The music and Elvis's hip-swinging jig stopped for the vows.

"Do you promise to polish each other's blue suede shoes?" Elvis asked.

We agreed.

"Do you promise to walk each other's hound dogs?" Elvis asked.

"I'm more of a cat person," I said. "But sure."

"Yes, yes to everything, Elvis!" Emir insisted.

Elvis asked for the rings. Emir said we didn't have them yet, that they were still at the engraver's. It was another detail that passed us by in the haste of arranging this wedding. I waited for the weight of this moment, the suspicion, but it passed without consequences. Such were the unforeseen advantages of getting married in Las Vegas—nothing is strange.

"In that case," Elvis said, "you may kiss the bride."

This was it. The time had come. Here we go. My stomach dropped, filled with apprehension and dread. More than anything, it was *this* that I was most nervous about. It hit me that *this*, not the exchange of vows, was what I had been dreading. The kiss. I squirmed. Time slowed as Emir and I leaned in. That sexual attraction had no part in our relationship was largely what made me feel confident, secure, and all right with doing

this. It was so lovely: to be married—yet to be free! All the
security of having a husband or partner with none of the requisite obligations. Dipping our feet into the shallow end. The
vows were light, their hound-dog-and-blue-suede-shoes nature
meant Emir and I never had to tell a lie about our intentions.
The kiss I'd so dreaded turned out to be even lighter.

The nervous anticipation was far worse than the actual moment
of the quick peck that was simultaneously our first kiss and our
last. And with that, Emir and I were officially linked by the state
of Nevada. We posed for photos with the minister and Elvis,
our INS photo album already coming together. Omar joined us
for some of them. As the three of us emerged from the chapel,
Elvis, the minister, and the receptionist waved and threw rice.

My married life would be one where the men were gay,
the nights late, and the word "settle" meant hooking up with

someone I didn't consider attractive (i.e., I settled for that loser from the Valley last night because I wore beer goggles), rather than down payments and giving up birth control (i.e., my husband and I settled down in the Valley).

At the Stratosphere, the Space Needle–shaped hotel casino, we ascended to The Big Shot: the world's highest thrill ride! thrill seekers only! That was us. the big shot shoots you, at 45 mph, from the 921-foot level to the 1,081-foot level in 2.5 seconds . . . then lets you free-fall back to the launching pad. you hit 4 g's on the way up and then 0 g's as you float out of your seat on the way down.

Here was the physical manifestation of what we had just done. We shot through the night, the wind deafening, the view magnificent and terrifying all at once. It hit me that I was strapped in and there was no getting off. I was in a free fall and there was nothing I could do but yield to gravity, submit to this machine. Going up is scary, coming down fun. Or was it the other way around? You realize you did something potentially crazy, experienced the thrill of it, and survived. When Omar, Emir, and I actually went on the ride, though, I screamed and screamed as we fell over the concentrated desert lights, that neon huddle of fireflies. It was over before I opened my eyes.

In the photograph of us, purchased on touchdown, Omar, furthest to the left, throws up his arms and wears a bemused smile, as if saying he had no responsibility in the matter. Then comes me, clutching the straps that hold my body to the machinery, my eyes clamped shut as tight as a newborn kitten's, my mouth open as far as it could be, screaming as if there were no safety belt, as if I were free-falling toward certain demise amongst the glittering lights. Then Emir, who is looking up, smart Emir, who looks up to avoid looking down. There are four seats on the ride, so to the right of Emir is a black man who is smiling as if he's having the best time in the world. He makes for a nice element in the photograph: a stranger, someone we don't know and will never see again who has unwittingly been captured in our memory.

Omar left us after that. He may as well have said "my work here is done," and lifted off into the sky like a superhero. In reality he went to search for a gay club. Emir and I went to the Hard Rock Casino, and after we were down to a few hundred dollars out of the thousand Mohammad had given us, we walked past the slots with no intention of playing. I dropped a quarter into a Jefferson Airplane White Rabbit Slot Machine as we made our way out and kept walking. "One pill makes you larger/ and one pill makes you small/ and the ones that mother gives you/ don't do anything at all . . ." The slot machine went crazy. We spun around. Three white rabbits.

We'd hit the jackpot.

Back in our room at the Motel 6, Emir and I crawled into our adjacent double beds a bit tipsy and too wired for sleep. We recounted the night to each other, laughing about the Elvis costume, our marriage license mishap, Omar's ostentatious ways, and the lucky slot machine win. When we finally exhausted our stories, I pulled *The Brothers Karamazov* from my purse and Emir took his Harry Potter hardcover from the nightstand. I found my place. We sat up reading in bed until it was time for lights-out.

# 6.

## Origin Story

"The future always looks good in the golden land,
because no one remembers the past." —Joan Didion

In the morning, Omar wanted to scalp tickets to the Britney
Spears concert, but I couldn't spend even one more second in
Las Vegas. It was up to Emir to make the call. The three of us got
into Emir's car, Omar muttering in the backseat about missing
the concert as I thought, *The wife wins out.* I was eager to get
home. Days on the Vegas Strip are like drinks: a certain amount
yields a pleasant buzz, but one too many and you start to feel
a little sick. Still, my state of mind was optimistic and hopeful.
*Well, that was easy. What next?*

It was the beginning of an adventure, performance art, a
statement. I felt fearless, even . . . *fierce*, certain that the next two
years were going to be stable, smooth sailing. I'd always have
Emir to count on. And I was going to learn so much: being

married to Emir was a unique opportunity as a training ground in being someone's partner, sans the passion that accompanied sexual relationships, which would allow me a sort of detached objectivity on the marriage act. Given the absence of passion and sex maybe I could at least wrap my mind around that. I'd wade in slowly and see if I couldn't figure out enough about marriage to feel confident entering one in the future, should that be the outcome.

In the apartment that was now ours, Emir and I curled up under a fuzzy gray blanket on the couch to watch more *Sex and the City*. I joked that I was guilty of "alien snuggling." Emir was the one person who laughed at my lame puns. That night, I drifted in and out of sleep, The Big Mom in the Sky on my mind. She didn't need to watch from the sky to find out I was married to Emir. All she had to do was type his name into the Consular Consolidated Database system at work. And if she did? Then what? I kept coming back to the question. Was she more Visa Chief than mother? *She loves me—she wouldn't out me as an alien smuggler, if that was even what I was. Would she?*

My mother was fond of reminding me I lacked judgment because my frontal lobe wasn't fully developed, that it would not be until I was twenty-five, and so I should avoid making any more major decisions until then. What if, blinded by passion, I married the wrong man? She was speaking from experience.

My father received his green card through his marriage to my mother but never sought U.S. citizenship. Carl Jung wrote that when an inner situation is not conscious, it appears in our lives as fate. My father, though still alive, was already a ghost.

After Emir and I were married, when things settled down

and the gravity of what we had done—what we were doing, for the journey had only just commenced—settled in, the thought crossed my mind that I might be attempting to compensate for something, or someone, buried deep in the past. Is it ever possible to escape carrying on family traditions, even unintentional ones?

All superheroes have origins, which are often not revealed until later in their narrative. I imagine my mother in a red cape, the letters VC imprinted in bright yellow or blue. The Visa Chief had a whole other life before her high-powered career. If she did find out I married Emir, I hoped she would understand because she had once been in a similar boat—literally, a ship. Her marriage to my father originated in deception, too. Whereas my lie was one of concealment, hers was overt. She needed help from her parents to marry my father so she could immigrate him to the United States. She wasn't marrying him for his green card, but she had to get him one if they were going to live together in Seattle, where she was from. She needed her birth certificate sent to Italy, but how would she get her parents to send it? He wasn't Jewish, he wasn't wealthy, he didn't have an established position in society—he worked in restaurants on transatlantic ships. He didn't even spend most of his time on solid ground. He was often at sea. She had to fabricate a story to hide who her husband-to-be really was from her parents. Sound familiar?

My mother had a comfortable childhood as the daughter of a doctor and a housewife. My grandfather's affairs were well-kept secrets to everyone except my grandmother, who turned a blind eye for years in a failed attempt at keeping her husband with her, keeping the family together. After forty years of marriage, many of them spent ignoring infidelity, she divorced him.

Anything my mother set out to do, she accomplished, and she raised me to believe I could do the same. As a teenager, my mother wanted to hang out with the Beatles. When the band came to Seattle, she made a stained glass window of the four of them with the Space Needle in the background, and after it was photographed for the newspaper, she went to the concert and gave it to them personally—and then hung out with them backstage. After years at an all-girls' school, my mother became adventurous and wild in her early twenties. When she went to Stanford, she bought a motorcycle. She used to hitchhike on private jets, drive to the airport with friends and see who was going where and how to get back. She returned to the University of Washington to finish her undergraduate degree, where her parents could keep a closer eye on her, at least until she escaped again, to graduate school, and then off to Italy for a summer program in Italian language and history. On the ship from New York City to Genoa, she met Gioacchino Giovanni Gennatiempo, the man who, five years later, would become my father. Unlike with Emir and me, there was traditional romance involved, a romance of cinematic proportions.

In 1974, Penny was twenty-three years old and enrolled in the PhD program in languages that would take her to Italy for a summer. She owned an orange MGB convertible—its slogan was "The Great Escape Car" and she was making her own great escape; an Italophile since the age of sixteen when she went on a high school program called The Experiment in International

Living, she was returning to the country she loved, the place where she felt she should have been born.

My mother wanted to take the car to Italy, which meant traveling by ship, the SS *Leonardo da Vinci*, from New York City to Genoa. On the ship, she met a handsome maitre d' with a long, complicated Italian name. Giovanni was thirty-five, a bachelor, and a wanderer.

It seems fitting to me now that their romance began at sea. There they were, on a boat together for two weeks, neither able to exit. Over those two weeks traversing the Atlantic, they fell in love, or at least into passion. I imagine them atop that vessel, kissing on the deck at night, drinking wine, and dancing at the top-floor disco.

"I'll bet you have a wife and kid waiting for you on the dock," she said one evening as they neared the port in Genoa. I imagine they were both dreading their moment of parting by then, not wanting the ship to ever anchor.

"*Te ho detto, non sono sposato,*" Giovanni said. *I told you, I'm not married.*

She never attended the summer program—students and professors across Italy were on strike; classes weren't being held. It was very Italian, *il sciopero*. She spent that time with her Italian love instead. Three months later, she wanted to bring him to America. Originally, my parents did not plan on getting married, at least not right away. My father went to an interview at the U.S. consulate. He was seeking a tourist visa so he could spend some time in the States with his new love and see if Seattle was for him. The visa officer, someone with the same job my mother would eventually have herself, denied him. Judging from my father's lack of financial stability, the likelihood that he would stay in the States and work illegally seemed high. The only other option to get him into the country was marriage.

If the visa interview had a different outcome, I wouldn't be writing this now. I wouldn't have existed at all. I guess I owe that visa officer my life.

My mother called her parents in Seattle and asked them to send her birth certificate to Italy so that she could marry Giovanni.

"No!" my grandfather protested over the phone. "You aren't even studying. You're definitely not getting married. You're to come home at once."

"If you don't send it, I'll never come home again."

"Who is this man?" my grandmother asked.

"He's the *Marchese di Monferrato*, Mom! An aristocrat descended from a long line of Italian royals."

"He's not even Jewish, for crying out loud!" my grandfather shouted.

He wasn't royalty—far from it. When my father was born, he was strapped to a board so his spine would grow straight. It did. He grew over six feet tall, and took after his father's Southern Italian side, darkly handsome. The rest of the family was farmers; he was the accomplished one for getting a degree from hospitality school and working on the ships.

*Marchese di Monferrato* was not an invention of my mother's imagination. The original marchese, Giovanni I, wrested control of Monferrato from Matteo Visconti, Lord of Milan, and his occupiers in 1303. Giovanni II, *Marchese di Monferrato*, defeated the Queen of Naples's troops in Gamenario in 1345. In 1378, Giovanni III took over *Marchese di Monferrato*–hood. Perhaps my mother learned about these *marcheses* in her graduate school Italian history classes. She based the fiction she created around my father in some form of truth. The Giovannis all shared a name. In Italian, the word *storia* means both "history" and "fiction." To know which genre a *storia* belongs to, you have to ask. What could I really know for sure about my mother's life before I was born? *La storia,* only *la storia.*

My grandparents, whether or not they believed the story, sent the birth certificate. My parents married in Genoa's city hall on February 17th, 1975. After the newlyweds moved back to Seattle, my father got his green card and my mother's parents found out he definitely wasn't a wealthy royal. All my grandmother would tell me was that by that point, they had no choice but to accept Giovanni the not-*marchese* into the family. The deed was done. If their daughter was happy, they would be, too. Besides, once Giovanni arrived in Seattle, his good looks and warm demeanor melted their resistant hearts, and they threw a lavish party to celebrate their daughter's marriage at the country club where my grandfather golfed. Giovanni was used to waiting on people like these on the ship; suddenly he found himself welcomed among them. And yet, in many ways he was still at sea. Always was. *Fish out of water,* as my grandmother called him.

On so many levels, our family histories seem to inform and influence our personal histories. The chance to give Emir the opportunity to succeed by helping him stay in the country where he could make his dreams come true—especially when I believed in him so much, in his talent as a screenwriter—could be seen as my subconscious attempt to make up for my father's failure to make something of his life in America. Growing up moving between different countries and cultures had taught me to be open-minded and birthed an interest in making the world smaller. Instead of trying to get a job at the U.N., I had done this. I was more interested in the small scale, the personal. Was it coincidence that my mother lied to her parents about who my father was, and I had entered a marriage that was kept secret from her? Was rebellion in our blood, or was I somehow repeating parts of her story? It was oddly coincidental that she had once done something deceptive in relation to marriage when she was my age, too. The insistence, the necessity: I'm doing this no matter what. There will be hard times, new beginnings, other loves, stupid mistakes, illnesses, travails you cannot foresee or imagine, but this much I can promise: I am keeping you with me.

'Til death, or divorce, do us part.

Part II:

# Keeping You With Me

# 7.

## If You Lived Here You'd Be Real by Now

In the weeks leading up to the wedding, my focus was entirely on the big day itself. Thinking of tying the knot as the main event made it easier not to contemplate what would happen afterward, which was a big open space. The marriage itself would last two years—minimum—and it lay ahead then, unfurling before us, filled with danger and possibility. We had gone through with it and I suddenly felt as committed as I was. Yet as a married woman, I was still the same young, lost, and love-hungry girl. With Emir, at least I wouldn't worry about the day he would pack his bags and walk out the door.

Through marriage to Emir, I was cheating what I saw as my certain fate of ending up a divorcée. By fulfilling this destiny, I became convinced I had turned the curse on its head, since when Emir and I divorced it would be a celebratory occasion. He would have his green card and be able to stay in America.

I could go on to marry for life with my newfound good marriage karma. Spending at least the next two years married to Emir also guaranteed I would not rush into marriage with the next man who would have me, as I had been so eager to do had I found someone, post-Julian, who was willing.

Emir and I had an album's worth of photographs of us from before we knew we would get married, photographs of us together when we were nineteen. I thought the process would be straightforward because what was there to fake or lie about? Only questions about our sex life would necessitate speaking untruths. Would they ask? It sounded uncomfortable—*so, how many times a week do you do it?*—delivered in the flat tone of a bureaucrat. Even that would only equate to a lie of omission, given that we each did have sex, just not with each other. But would our argument hold up at the INS? It was no joke— deportation and being permanently barred from the United States for him; hefty fines and jail time for me. And yet before this it already felt as if he was my family. Emir *was* family. We just made it official.

Still, we already knew that come the judgment day of our INS interview, we weren't going to take any risks. We wouldn't mention a thing about Emir's sexuality. We would hold hands tightly. Amorously. Advice from our lawyer. Twenty-two years old and we had a lawyer. We had done something so much bigger than we were, something that merited a *lawyer*. This was beyond Intro to Adulthood 101.

The lawyer, Lilah, was a lesbian who was also from Emiristan. She was as short as I was and sported a pixie haircut, striped button-down shirt, khakis, and penny loafers. The Emiristani community in L.A. was a small one, and Emir heard Lilah was uniquely qualified. She had worked on these kinds of cases before. So there were others out there, others like us, I realized, though it seems obvious now that we couldn't have been the only gay/straight best friends to get married to keep someone from leaving. I imagined all the combinations of couples that were surely out there. We could start an underground club.

Lilah's office became a place we would go to sign forms with cryptic combinations of letters and numbers, paperwork I didn't bother to read through. I scrawled my name and everything was sent for processing. My signature on a piece of paper, and checks Emir wrote—this was all it took. It felt not much more complicated than adopting a puppy.

When I came home one evening and found Emir on the couch in tears, I immediately assumed the worst: an immigration-related scenario. Something had gone wrong with our paperwork. I dropped my things and ran over to where he was crumpled on the couch. Had Emir been right? Was our paperwork rejected? Were we being watched? Paranoid thoughts scrolled through my head like a news ticker. He didn't look up at me when I sat beside him and put a hand on his back.

"What's the matter, what happened?" I asked.

"Adrian broke up with me."

Adrian. Our paths crossed only on occasion—either our schedules conflicted or we were moving around each other warily, not wanting to jockey for center stage in Emir's life.

Adrian was thirty-four and resembled Emir's first boyfriend, Carey. Carey was from Boston but had grown up overseas because of his father's job, and one of the places he lived as a teen was Emiristan. Carey still spoke the language, knew the customs, was familiar with the neighborhood in which Emir grew up. Who knew, maybe they even passed each other on the street? They were joined at the hip for almost a year before Carey met someone else and broke it off. Emir was devastated.

Now it had happened again and I was devastated.

Through his tears, Emir explained that Adrian left him for someone else—someone younger. *Younger?* I was shocked. "How young?"

Over the last five months of their relationship, Adrian had been chatting online with a seventeen-year-old boy from a fundamentalist evangelical home in Kentucky. When he turned eighteen, Adrian invited him to move to West Hollywood, to run away and live with him, which he did. Emir was caught by surprise and humiliated. We nicknamed Adrian's new boyfriend The Kid, as if he had a walk-on part in a movie and was undeserving of a name. But it wasn't The Kid's fault.

*You think you know someone,* Emir and I said to each other.

"You think you know him, that he loves you the way you love him, and then he goes and does something like this," I said, though I myself had gone and done something like this, too, and had no idea why I should be so shocked. "You thought at least you could expect honesty but even that is too difficult sometimes for some people. Sometimes those people are others, other times it's us."

We wanted authenticity, something real, someone who would be there, we said. Things like this happen, and it's so easy to give up, to say you want to write off relationships even though you already know you don't mean it and you won't, that as soon as the next one pops up you will be right back there again. The heart's memory is short. What hurt Emir most was that he and Adrian had been talking about what the next step in their relationship should be. They couldn't move in together because Emir was marrying me, and Emir wondered if that provoked the Kid thing, if Adrian felt pushed away or uncomfortable with the marriage.

Having a partner made it easier to take a chance on the uncertain. So did our already having taken the biggest risk of our lives by getting married. I still felt the pull of New York City, the path not taken. Emir agreed: a fresh start for newly-weds was in order. This was something we could do together, something more easily done together, sparing us the anxiety of moving to Manhattan alone to live in a small apartment with strangers. There was someone to navigate while you drove blindfolded. Moving together would be a huge exercise in trust and teamwork. It was also more proof for our INS packet. Couples in prototypical green card marriages didn't move across the country together, to a city where they would live in an apartment the size of a cubicle.

In New York, a city of immigrants and transients, we could easily blend in. Our files could be transferred to the INS office in downtown Manhattan—same plan, different city. I would be lying if I said I didn't think of Julian, that if only I could get him to see me, maybe there was still a chance. Even though

Emir was in favor of the new-life-in-New York idea, I worried that whatever I decided, he didn't have much of a choice. It felt strange to have such power over another person's fate. For at least the next two years Emir was coming with me. I didn't want to move him around as if he were a chess piece on a board, as my mother did my father and, for a longer stretch, me. This was not indentured servitude. There were no marionettes here.

"Don't move to New York," my mother said. "There's anthrax there. The whole city's a mess."

Five people had died of anthrax inhalation that fall but Emir and I were going and nothing was going to stop us. Emir didn't want to go on a cross-country road trip—motel sheets and rest-stop toilets were not for him. I tried to convince him there was no better way to see the country but he wasn't having it. I wanted to drive and he wanted to fly. We had reached the first impasse of our young marriage. Emir would stay behind to pack boxes and sell furniture while I hit the road; I would get there first and find an apartment, and then he would join me.

Before I left on the road trip, we ran errands for the marriage: adding me to Emir's bank account, filling out change of status forms. It had been so easy to immigrate Emir simply by promising to walk his hound dog and polish his blue suede shoes. He took the requisite medical exam that proved he tested negative for HIV, tuberculosis, and hepatitis A through C. At the time, HIV-positive travelers were not allowed into the country even on tourist visas. As for trying to immigrate to the U.S. if you were HIV-positive, it was not an option. The law forbade it. But Emir didn't have to worry about that. Aside from being underweight and a smoker, he was in perfect health.

Emir offered to pay the bills and a larger chunk of the rent in New York and I told him that was more than enough. We weren't really husband and wife. We were partners. In crime, perhaps.

The plan was straightforward, the route, winding. I drove up through Las Vegas, to the Hoover Dam and then back south, visiting the Grand Canyon, Sedona, White Sands in New Mexico, a town called Truth or Consequences. When I was a child, my mother and I traveled on weekends to medieval Italian mountain towns. She liked to say, "no one knows where we are," a glimmer in her eye, marveling and mischievous. She sought comfort in travel; she used it to escape. *No one knew where I was*, I often thought out on the open road. I wondered what I was trying to escape from.

Something strange happened in El Paso. Staring at the road atlas and seeing how little progress I had made, how all this driving was not what I thought, how I didn't feel wild and free but agoraphobic and terrified, I began to see what this really was: an inability to put down roots, to stay in one place, the very things I told myself I wanted so much. I was always running away. Struck by the feeling that running away was the motive for the move, I could not go forward. I started driving *back*, through winding roads in Northern Arizona, all the way back to Sedona, where I sat in a tarot studio and asked the matronly card reader where I really belonged: New York or L.A.? I remembered the night of September 10th, drawing tarot cards on the bedroom floor. The funny thing was I didn't completely believe in tarot. It was an intrigue, another way of getting to feel as though everything was already fated, a convenient way of avoiding self-implication because whatever happened was going to happen anyway.

"You have a Western soul," the tarot reader said, as if she were telling me the sky was blue or there were a lot of crystal shops in Sedona. "You belong in California." Well, that was that. I called Emir and told him I needed to come back. I hadn't thought this through. I couldn't do it alone.

"What? Why?" Emir asked.

I had a million excuses but not one good reason.

Angry with myself, I planned out my own punishment while I was still on the road. I spent another night in Sedona and rented a room in L.A. from a guy I had met in a diner once, who happened to have a posting on Craigslist. "Aren't you Cameron from that night at Fred 62's?" I'd written. What a coincidence, he replied. Of course, the room was mine if I wanted it. I didn't want to burden Emir with my presence and knew that as long as we had the same mailing address, filed taxes jointly, and had both our names on a bank account, we'd most likely be golden with the INS. My fear of rejection, that Emir would not love me anymore after my decision to move and then not to move, that he would hate me for dictating the circumstances of his life this way, prompted my leaving. I would go so he wouldn't have to live with my inadequacies, resent me, or feel bad about kicking me out.

The sky was clear, dotted with stars behind the streetlamps. I had gone out onto the open road only to return right here, as if L.A. were a magnet pulling me back. It was as if I had no choice in the matter—it wasn't a decision at all, but rather something that just happened, a course charted out, and I followed the footsteps. I hated that I had disappointed Emir and didn't even have a viable explanation for my odd behavior. I couldn't take the unusual quiet of the apartment. He gave me the silent treatment the night I got home.

"Can we go somewhere and talk?" I asked.

Emir shrugged and put on his sweatshirt. We walked down the street to Whole Foods on Santa Monica Boulevard and perused the salad bar in silence. I went to the cold bar and began assembling a salad as light pop music drowned out the silence between us. He wandered over to the hot food. We paid at separate registers and went outside to the picnic bench overlooking a sea of scattered cars. The Whole Foods parking lot glistened in the moonlight as if implanted with diamonds— there, but not for the taking. I jabbed a broccoli floret with a plastic fork. Emir didn't touch his samosas.

"Couldn't you have thought about it more?" he asked. "I mean, how could you not know you didn't want to go to New York until you were halfway through Texas?"

"El Paso isn't halfway through Texas."

"What is this, *Thelma & Louise*?"

"I'm sorry," I said. "It's not that I don't want to go to New York. Something just wasn't . . . right."

I was going to have to do better, I knew. Still, I had no explanation that would suffice. Had I decided too late to follow my mother's wishes? Was it fear, or a panic attack? All I did know for sure was that I felt like a directionless mess, couldn't handle commitment, and was jeopardizing Emir's safety. We had just married and I was already screwing up.

I told Emir he didn't need me around. I was unreliable. I had hurt him, ruined all our big plans, and could not be trusted. In order to try to understand, to get some perspective, I needed to retreat. I told him about having browsed for rooms to sublet on Craigslist, and that I would be moving out for a while, until I got my head on straight.

Emir was shocked. "That's worse!" he protested. "We have to live together."

"My mail will come to your place. We'll still do the marriage thing, just like we planned. I'll be out of your hair."

"Living separately is asking for trouble!"

"It's only a trial separation . . . until you aren't mad at me anymore. We can even work it into our story. They might ask us if we ever went through a hard time or something. Or what the hardest time we faced as a couple was. You know . . . something."

Emir insisted I was wrong, that I was subconsciously trying to sabotage our marriage. Yes, he was angry, but it would pass, we could talk through it, come up with a new plan, save money, and move to New York down the line. My moving out was taking things too far. He was not going to ask me to leave. No, no, I insisted. I'd messed up, I didn't deserve to come home.

Emir slapped his forehead. He was exasperated with me and so was I, so I moved into Cameron's with the two suitcases packed in my trunk from the road trip. At least one of us would not have to deal with me for a while. It must have been terrifying for Emir to have to wonder whether or not I would be able to keep it together enough to carry this off, or whether my volatility might lead to his deportation.

Two weeks later, Cameron announced he reunited with his girlfriend and told me he was very sorry to have to ask me to leave, but she was moving back in. The breakup was the reason he decided to get a roommate. Luckily for me, Emir welcomed me back, if not exactly with open arms, at least with a wry half-smile. He came to Cameron's house and helped me pack again.

And so Emir and I came back together, taking a fresh start only a month into our newlywed life. This thing with the move, it was only a little blip, a momentary lapse of reason. It would be smooth sailing from here on out. Emir had accepted my apology, and the coast was clear. We settled into a state of cautious ease in the little apartment on Havenhurst Drive.

I changed my address at the post office and my last name at the DMV. Emir didn't ask me to change my name but I was more connected to Emir than my father and I knew that bearing Emir's name would look good for the INS. Early in the morning, sun peeking through the smoggy haze, the lines for the INS building were already around the block. The office was still overwhelmed by Iranians registering as required by post-9/11 regulations. Los Angeles has one of the largest Iranian communities outside of Tehran and it seemed as if everyone had come to sign in at once.

Emir waited nervously to file his Application to Adjust Status, Form I-485. Anyone whose status was questionable in any way, no matter how slight, was detained on the spot, in that very building. Nothing about us was questionable, I repeated—student visa, college sweetheart, marriage. There were no blips in his background, nothing that rendered him suspicious in any way . . . well, other than his effeminate mannerisms, which were what worried us most—that Emir was obviously gay and even if he tried to hide it, it still might be clear enough to raise suspicions.

That day, though, he made it through the very first step in our journey, no questions asked, and he was soon after able to file his Application for Employment Authorization, Form I-765, after which he received his Employment Authorization Document. Emir could then work legally in the United States pending our INS interview, which, if all went well, would grant him the green card, and after two years of marriage the green card would become permanent, so he would be able to stay in the country even if we decided to get a divorce. Even then, I could only imagine the divorce would happen if and when I got serious enough with another man, and maybe even then only after that man proposed. If that never happened, I could stay married to Emir 'til death do us part; the only reason to divorce would be another marriage.

Without the urgency of having to find a permanent full-time job to sponsor his work visa, Emir decided to work odd jobs and dedicate his mental energy to writing screenplays, the dream we once shared that I had since given up on.

Emir found a job at an upscale Italian restaurant on Sunset

owned by a Lebanese expat. (Though he could probably have worked there under the table, he now needn't fear *la migra*.) We mirrored my parents yet again. Emir also took a second part-time job, selling spa packages on the streets of Beverly Hills. That one only paid commission but the schedule was flexible.

Emir started a second screenplay and wrote a spec episode for *Will & Grace* that also placed among the finalists in a teleplay competition. His work was doing well, but no bites in terms of agents or sales. One agent he met with told him that "gay doesn't pay," and that he should turn his gay romantic comedy into a straight one, with a strong female supporting role. Emir refused and the agent wished him luck.

While Emir was discovering the joys of freelancing, I was growing weary of constantly calling connections to ask about upcoming jobs, the perpetual search for gigs. The production designer I worked for didn't have anything for me; business was tanking along with the economy. Every day brought news of another Screen Actors Guild strike, and work in film production became even harder to find than usual. My resume consisted of a list of freelance art department jobs on commercials and low-budget movies, including a soft-core porn, *Embrace the Darkness II,* a film featuring exotic vampire sex scenes. During the shoot, I spent my days painting sets in a basement, grateful to be far from the action. Since then I had been craving routine, a predictable day, happy hour with happy coworkers, fluorescent lighting, cubicles, and complicated office phones with alien ring tones and all. After embracing the darkness, I began applying for every conceivable entertainment industry position set in an office: talent agency assistant, script development assistant, advertising and public relations assistant. I was ready to do anything.

They'd just put up the Christmas decorations, tinsel in Tinseltown. One-dimensional gold bells and shiny green wreaths decked out Hollywood Boulevard. Emir and I spent hours sitting on the white Ikea couch together, drinking coffee and tea, playing backgammon, and talking. I applied for jobs and Emir wrote. Sometimes I wrote, too—short stories about girls in their early twenties in L.A. looking for love. These were the most thinly veiled of fictions, cathartic, confessional, and self-indulgent. They were more akin to a diary than anything, but writing was a way of salvaging odd moments from what would otherwise be lost. I sought shelter in the communal solitude of coffee shops with every other aspiring writer in L.A. I wrote about the matching tattoos Julian and I had gotten. And I wrote about Elise and Ahmed, a young woman and her gay best friend who got married for his green card. It did not work as fiction.

8.

Domestic Blips

After I applied to hundreds of entertainment industry desk jobs, out of the void came a solitary response: an interview for a position in a talent agency's mailroom. The agency occupied the twenty-fifth floor of a Century City office tower, the only skyscraper I'd set foot in since moving to Los Angeles. The office was all steel and glass, spare, modern, and minimalist. Sharks swam in shallow waters. Dorothy, the human resources manager, led me around to the offices of various agents who asked impromptu questions. Behind their heads was a panoramic view of Beverly Hills and, on the other side of the floor, Santa Monica, all the way out to the ocean. I wondered about earthquakes. I must have been mailroom material because Dorothy called the next day and offered me the job.

The first order of business was to fill out paperwork. I'd never had to check the Married box before. My pen-gripping hand instinctively went for the single box and I caught myself right in time, *Wait, I'm married. Right.*

On the Emergency Contact portion of the form, I scribbled Emir's name. Relationship to Employee: *soul mate.*

Dorothy scanned the forms to make sure I had filled everything out.

"Honey, you checked the Married box, right here, see?" she said.

"Right. Because I'm married. He's my emergency contact, too."

"Oh, I see. I apologize . . . I thought you checked the wrong box—you're so young!"

"We get that all the time," I said and smiled. "My husband and I met in college. We moved out here together."

"Don't wear a ring?" she asked, eyeing my left hand.

"We're saving up for them."

Damn I'm good at this, I thought. Too good. Should that worry me? I wanted honesty but defaulted toward deception.

If I told my co-workers I had a gay roommate and it got back to Dorothy, or if Dorothy mentioned my husband and I'd told people I was single, the story would not add up. Emir and I hadn't decided on an official story to tell people in our daily lives. We were still planning to date, to carry out these daily lives as if we were best friends and roommates, not a couple. We didn't want potential romantic prospects to think us unavailable, so we would not wear rings. Emir planned to buy those sometime before our interview, but we saw no need for them until then. Maybe we were wrong.

I decided to say I had a husband and a gay roommate. Emir

could be two people at once, like a superhero with a secret identity.

My training involved learning where the postage machine was and how it worked, where the headshots were filed, and how to put calls through from the reception desk, which I would occasionally cover on lunch hour. The job was easy and required little effort but I made it difficult for myself. The Big Mom in the Sky was a voice inside my head: *Impress people! Show them how brilliant you are, how special, how they should promote you to agent in your first month!* I didn't want to be an agent but my perception of what it meant to have a job was that you did something you didn't want to do all day and that was why you got paid. I learned it from her. My mother loved traveling and living abroad. She was less passionate about being a bureaucrat; she complained about work, but she still tried to outdo all of her peers, to win the most awards, and to be the most respected and accomplished in her field. "I don't want to work in an office," I told her when I was a kid and we talked about what I wanted to do when I grew up.

"Well," she said. "Jobs are in offices."

"Not all jobs."

"All jobs worth having."

I was glad my art department assistant jobs mainly took place in my car, on the streets of Los Angeles, where my daily scavenger hunts included items such as Millennium Edition Evian water bottles, blacklight posters with figures demonstrating various sexual positions, and wall sconces. I retreated into an office because I was tired and didn't know what else to do. I felt listless. The wedding—the marriage—was a Band-Aid on

The Lack: my father, a lover, a deeper connection with another person or with myself, a desire to be seen, noticed, accomplished . . . to matter—things I didn't have or that were lost.

Back home after my first day in the mailroom, Emir and I made spaghetti and put candles on the table for a romantic dinner at home. The blinds on the floor-to-ceiling windows were open, and with the porch light on, the pool in the courtyard was illuminated and shimmering, dark water rippling in the yellow light. I loved our apartment; unlike others I'd lived in, it was clean and airy, an adult home. We took some pictures for our wedding album. I poured two glasses of white wine. As we sat down to eat and Emir asked me about my first day, the first thing I mentioned was checking the Married box.

"For your outside-the-box marriage," he joked.

"How should we do this? Now that I'm not freelance I'm going to see the same people every day . . . I'm not sure what to tell them—that I'm married? Or the truth? What if I want to date someone from work?"

"Don't shit where you eat," Emir said.

I laughed.

"I'm serious," he said. "We have to maintain appearances. There are so many people you don't work with that you could date. What if the INS sent someone over to your office?"

"That only happens in movies."

"Sweetie . . ."

"I won't say anything unless it comes up. Maybe Dorothy won't mention it."

I'd signed up for this. I knew what I'd bargained for, that the arrangement would entail a good deal of compromise.

Interoffice dating was a terrible idea anyway. Still, Emir's controlling side reminded me of my mother.

"It's just that I want to be in a relationship so bad," I said.

"Masturbation can only cut it for so long."

After dinner, I did the dishes and then Emir and I watched *The Object of My Affection*, which I reclassified as a horror movie after the scene where Jennifer Aniston's character, Nina, kisses her gay roommate, George, and starts taking off his shirt before he stops it from going further. Emir and I had a running joke that if neither of us ever met anyone else and my biological clock was ticking away, we could have a child together via artificial insemination.

What I did appreciate in *The Object of My Affection* was protagonist Nina's comment to her stepsister, asking if she and her husband still had sex. We learned that the frequency and intensity of sex fades in all intimate relationships over time. I noted it down for my defense-of-Emir-marriage list.

"WHO TAUGHT YOU HOW TO WASH DISHES?" Emir blared from the kitchen.

"What's the matter with the dishes?"

"There are still bits of food stuck to these! It's disgusting!"

I picked up plates and inspected them. "They look clean to me."

"Look at this place! The countertops sparkle and you leave coffee-cup rings everywhere. My clothes are folded and hanging up, you trail them everywhere and leave piles on the bathroom floor."

"Fine, so I rushed through the dishes. But I'm doing you a huge favor!"

As soon as I spoke those words, I was hit in the chest by regret. Emir groaned, walked into the living room, and flipped the television back on. I ran out after him.

"Are you going to do this every time?" he said. "'Emir, I did you a huge favor, wash the dishes! Emir, I did you a huge favor, do the laundry!' Did you do it because you want a slave, someone to dote on you while you do whatever you want?"

"Of course not," I said.

The room was too cold. Emir kept the air-conditioning going full blast and I couldn't stand it. I took a sweatshirt I'd hung over the back of a chair and put it on, zipped it up to the neck. "It's not like you're perfect, you know," I said. "You keep that box on twenty-four seven." I pointed at the TV. "Did you ever think I might like some quiet around here? Or for the air conditioner to be off sometimes?"

"Then why didn't you say so? Why did you wait until it bothered you so much?"

Why *didn't* I say so?

"I guess it's that I'm not used to having anyone to 'say so' to," I said.

I turned off *The Golden Girls* and sat down next to Emir. Our first married argument, I pointed out. And it was just like any married argument, about dishes and cleaning and living together. Even *we* slipped into learned male–female behavior. Our first married argument was a typical lovers' quarrel—born from a lack of communication. Emir hadn't mentioned that what I was doing (or not doing) bothered him until it boiled over and he snapped.

"We have to raise issues the second they come up. Tension comes from what's left unsaid," I told him.

"Okay, you're right," he said. "Here's my first married apology. I'm sorry I yelled at you."

"I need you to know that I would never want you to feel indebted to me. I didn't do this because I wanted a housekeeper."

"I know that, or I wouldn't have said yes. I trusted you and for some reason, I still do."

A month into my job at the agency, I earned authorization to do mail runs. At designated intervals throughout the day, senior members of the mailroom staff were sent out into the wilds of the agency to distribute incoming mail and messenger packages. No one spoke to me other than to thank me, and I didn't have to speak other than "have a nice day," "you got it," and "no problem." It was a good place to be anonymous. I went through my days wearing gray suits, driving into the garage at seven each morning, delivering mail, and answering the phone when the receptionist went to lunch.

I noticed Oliver during an early mail run over to the literary department, the screenwriters' agents' domain. Oliver was bookish and badass at the same time, with a mop of brown hair, black-framed glasses, and a chronically pensive yet mischievous expression on his face. He seemed to be an adventurer, a man with secrets. I could tell he was a wanderer, too. (*Among wolves we recognize ourselves*, a friend who wasn't a native English speaker once said to me. Despite the odd phrasing, the meaning was entirely clear, and the line came back to me whenever I was struck by that feeling of familiarity with someone I had just met.)

I lived for those mail runs to Oliver, cute Oliver with his black-rimmed glasses and thick brown hair that waved down into his eyes, sweet Oliver with his quiet and intense demeanor, intellectual Oliver who read the classics at his desk when the phones were quiet, brilliant Oliver whom I fantasized about pulling into the maintenance closet with me when we worked after hours or seducing at our office happy hour. He seemed out of place at the agency, too. All the other assistants wore sleek suits and crafted personas—young sharks, mini-versions of their bosses. Oliver looked more like a budding literature professor with his elbow-padded jackets. Oliver loved books more than anything, which meant I loved him more than anything, even books.

Some nights, I drove up and down Wilshire Boulevard past Oliver's apartment after finding the address in the internal company directory. I hoped to catch a glimpse of Oliver through a window or, better yet, on the sidewalk outside. I didn't know what I expected to achieve this way or what I planned to say if I did run into him. Oliver was out of my league. I didn't imagine he could see me even when I was standing right in front of his desk. Typical of a bookish type, he seemed absentminded, focused on private thoughts. Emir had asked me not to get involved with anyone at the office, the only rule we'd established in our marriage so far, but I was inching closer. Maybe that's why I had to do it—because someone told me not to.

One evening, during an office outing at a British-style pub called The Cat & Fiddle, I worked up the courage to sit down at Oliver's table and try to flirt. I asked him questions; he was from the East Coast, had majored in literature, wanted to go back to school for a PhD in the Nineteenth Century. I decided to tell him about Emir; the story would make me more interesting. But as I began, a sweep of my hand knocked my wineglass over onto Oliver's lap instead, staining his pressed khakis. He looked down at the stain and then up at me, saying nothing. He cocked an eyebrow.

I apologized over and over and handed Oliver napkins. We finished sopping up the wine and I apologized again, finally daring to look up at Oliver. I was surprised to see him smiling.

"Don't worry about it," he said.

"You'll send me the dry-cleaning bill."

"I have ten more pairs of pants exactly like these."

"I'm so, so sorry," I repeated.

"It's nothing." He dabbed his lap with the napkins some more. "So, what were you saying?"

I smiled back. Oliver was kind. I told him I was married and as soon as the disappointed look registered—and I, in turn, registered the look was one of disappointment—I told him to whom. It was a spontaneous and naïve confession, prompted by a desire to get the object of my fixation, my Oliver, to notice me. "Accidentally" telling a virtual stranger what was supposed to be my greatest secret was an irresponsible mistake, one of my first in the time Emir and I were married. I jeopardized everything just to get noticed by Oliver. I shouldn't have mentioned it at all, but at the time, having the complete, enraptured attention of the usually aloof Oliver put me in an awestruck state. I wanted him to think I was even a fraction as intriguing as he was to me. Rather than trying to backtrack, I went further in, adding the part about what my mother did for a living. Oliver's eyebrows arched.

"That's quite a story," he said.

*I love you*, I thought. But the story didn't win him over. For weeks our relationship played out only within the confines of my mind.

Before I could make any progress with Oliver, my mother flew into town for a visit.

"I'm taking you and Emir out to a nice dinner when I get there."

My mother's generous offer to take us to a restaurant we couldn't otherwise afford would not have been cause for a panicked frenzy under typical circumstances. The night before her arrival, Emir and I scurried around the apartment like squirrels preparing for winter. We buried banking paperwork bearing both our names, photographs of us with the red-suited Elvis impersonator, and Emir's I-485 forms. My mother had only to see the code I-485 to know what we had done, and we worried she would sniff us out like a German shepherd and fifty-two tons of cocaine at baggage claim.

She'd gone on a business trip to Tijuana and then to Seattle to see my grandmother. She was stopping by on her way back out of the country, staying at The Standard hotel. It would be Penny's first time meeting Emir in person. They had spoken over the phone before, even at length, and they got on well. My mother knew Emir as my good friend from college and she was glad I had a "nice roommate." How was it possible that these two had never met before?

Then she was in our apartment, standing in our living room, wearing a red belted dress and hugging me. She smelled of L'Air du Temps and had a short haircut with chunky blonde highlights.

At Chaya Brasserie in Mid-City, Los Angeles, my mother told us about new border security and visa procedures, how a lack of interagency communication led to the September 11th attacks. Billions of dollars were being invested in new border surveillance technologies; Canada was problematic. Closed borders with the U.S. would be disastrous for Mexico.

"Nothing could have prepared us for this," my mother said. "How is the wine?"

"Good," we said, nodding in unison.

"What people need to understand now is that terrorism and immigration enforcement are different things."

"That's a great point," Emir said, and I agreed.

Maybe my mother wouldn't disown me if she found out about our marriage. Maybe I wasn't going against the system but helping it along. Helping it run more efficiently. As much as I liked that notion, I knew even then it was wishful thinking that my mother would be anything but appalled.

"Why don't you get the scallops," she said. I wanted fish but so did she, and how would we trade bites if we ordered the same thing? To me, scallops were the seafood equivalent of sneezed-on marshmallows. Nothing's viler than a scallop. But my mother wanted me to order them. When your mother is my mother and she wants you to order scallops, you order scallops.

Also, if you are married to your best friend for his green card and your mother is an immigration expert, and if you are out to dinner with both, *don't go to the bathroom*. When the two are left alone together, without you as a reliable buffer to steer the conversation *away* from green card, border crossing, and immigration, these topics will surely come up, as it's something the two of them have in common. Back in September, before Emir agreed to marry me, I'd asked my mother all those questions about his visa problem and what could be done to keep my beloved friend from having to return to a country where being murdered for being gay was not considered a hate crime but a fine thing to do because homosexuals were subhuman creatures who purposefully went against the laws of nature.

Because I had asked these questions—and here was Emir—I returned to the table from the bathroom and sat down to the uncomfortable conversation already in progress.

"It hasn't expired yet," said Emir, shoveling a forkful of pasta into his mouth.

"But if you're freelance, who is sponsoring–?"

"Who would like another scallop?" I interrupted. "Mom? Scallop?"

My mother speared one, never diverting her focus from Emir. "Have you applied for asylum?" she asked.

"Yes," he lied.

"The system is so slow and it's backed up on top of that. I wish there were some way I could help you, but I can at least check on your case and give you some idea of when you might expect to hear . . ."

"Mom, he really doesn't need—"

"I have to use the . . . excuse me," said Emir, his face blanching. He walked across the crowded restaurant and disappeared into the restroom.

My mother reached over and speared another scallop. She lowered her voice to a whisper.

"Do you think he's lying?" she asked.

"Mom!"

"There's no *way* Emir isn't illegal now. His O-1 would have expired *months* ago and he says he's freelancing."

"I haven't looked through his file cabinet. It's none of my business. Or yours."

"It is your business, Lize. You live with him. Do you really know him? Do you know what his family does?"

"That's totally paranoid. I spend all my time with him. If he were up to anything sketchy, I would know, and please don't call me Lize."

"You've only known him for a couple of years."

"Who do *you* spend all your time with, Mom?" I was regressing, becoming more and more the acrimonious teenager by the second. "Maybe you need to get a life. Then you'd have something to focus your energy on instead of what my roommate is doing."

It was mean but I was angry and afraid. I put the last scallop in my nervous mouth.

"Is it possible he found an American and got married?"

There was only one way out. I remembered everything I possibly could from the one course I took on Method acting. My heart palpitated wildly, a fish out of water flopping helplessly in my chest. My breath caught in my windpipe. I knew these feelings from panic attacks I'd had in college. I clutched my throat as if my airway was blocked. My eyes bulged. I was choking on a scallop. Within moments, I felt arms encircling my belly. I had no idea Emir knew the Heimlich maneuver. What if our INS interviewer separated us and asked me if my husband knew the Heimlich maneuver? I would have said no!

The sad, distended scallop plopped on the restaurant floor like a rejected organ.

"You okay, sweetie?" Emir asked, handing me a glass of water.

I coughed, and breathed. My mother thanked Emir. I would never tell either I had fake-scallop-choked, and the conversation we'd been having prior to my Oscar-worthy performance was forgotten. I sipped the water cautiously, wiped my eyes with a napkin, and watched as the restaurant settled back down. Onlookers dispersed back to their tables.

Emir rubbed my back. We were safe, at least for the time being. Saved by the scallop.

I wished Emir and I had thought to come up with a story about some employer or something before my mother arrived. Why didn't we sit down to talk about it? It felt like self-sabotage. Of course this was going to come up, she was going to talk to him about his immigration status—why wouldn't she? We hadn't thought to have our story prepared; we had been so wrapped up in the narrative we would present to the INS that we didn't come up with a story for the woman who mattered most, who knew we were not college sweethearts, didn't get engaged in L.A., and most certainly were not in traditional-marriage-style love. So new to this strange version of marriage, in our naïveté we sabotaged ourselves by forgetting to create another reality for my mother, who now seemed suspicious that something was amiss. I silently prayed to the god I didn't believe existed but called upon during airplane takeoffs and after breakups. *Please, please, let her forget.*

She would be livid. Or worse: disappointed.

After dropping my mother off at The Standard, Emir and I went straight to the Abbey for Appletinis to take the edge off. The outdoor courtyard was emptier than usual. Maybe another neighborhood gay bar was screening the latest episode of *Sex and the City* or having half-priced specials. The venues we frequented had "nights"—drag night, ladies' night, discount Cosmo night.

"What was up at the restaurant?" he asked.

"What do you mean?" I asked, not wanting to tell him about the conversation he almost walked in on.

"I was more grilled than the fish," he said. "She knows something is up."

"No, she doesn't."

"If she suspects, she can easily find out."

"Right."

"What do we do?"

"What can we do?"

"Will she get me deported?"

"I don't know," I said, "but I don't think so."

"What should we do?"

"Sit tight. Hope for the best."

## 9.
## We're Like the Same Person

Oliver and I flirted at the office. I melted when he looked up at me and smiled as I rolled my mail cart through the literary department. We were meant to be, I could feel it. It was only a matter of time. He was handsome without being arrogant, quiet but not shy, literary, intelligent, and well-traveled. He was perfect for me. All I had to do was get him to realize it, too.

We went out for happy hour with a group of assistants and the mailroom kids. I made sure to sit next to Oliver. This was the evening he would realize that he and I were supposed to be together. We talked about books, art, the places we'd traveled and the places where we still wanted to go. Oliver smelled like fresh laundry and a hint of the whiskey he was sipping. As I listened to his stories I wanted to reach over and run my hands through his hair.

"I'm in love," I told Emir.

"With Oliver?"

"He's amazing."

"He's someone from work. Remember what we agreed?"

"We don't get to choose who we fall in love with."

"And you promised no one from work. Don't shit where you eat—remember?"

"I already told him about us and he is totally cool with it."

"Oh, God."

Emir put his head in his hands.

"Don't be paranoid, honey. It's fine."

"Is it? Between your mother and this I am a little worried."

"It's going to be fine."

Before anything could happen between Oliver and me, a mail-room cohort heard that Oliver was sleeping with another assistant at the agency: a tall, thin blonde with big blue eyes, creamy alabaster-doll skin, and perfectly plucked brows. She wore makeup and dressed in colors and patterns. It made sense now, why I saw them leaving for lunch together, why she hung around his desk. I'd somehow convinced myself they were just good friends.

Though Oliver hadn't promised me anything and certainly didn't owe me anything, I felt betrayed, as if he should have admitted up-front he was involved with someone, someone from the office no less, for no other reason than it was obvious I was interested and pursuing him. Instead, he lied by omission.

"If he told me, I wouldn't have let myself develop such

strong feelings for him," I whispered to Emir over the phone from the reception desk at lunch hour. "Where are you? It's so noisy."

"I'm on Rodeo Drive," he said. "Not even one sale today."

Emir was out selling spa packages.

It wasn't exactly his American dream come true, either.

I cyberstalked Oliver as if I could get closer to him that way. I lit candles and put the Coldplay album *Parachutes* on repeat to set the mood so I could lie on the floor with my laptop and a glass of wine and engage in a little innocent online lurking, since Oliver was so out of reach in real life.

What I found was an LAPD web page.

Featuring a mug shot.

I peered into his brown eyes and at the numbers my Oliver's hands held up to his chest, white on black. It was definitely him. I read the accompanying case history and then I read it again. Oliver was at one point wanted for stealing hundreds of valuable rare first-edition books, notably a copy of *Ulysses* that detectives were still "trying to locate." At the end of the article was the contact information for the detective at the Art Theft detail who was the point person for Oliver's case.

Oliver looked handsome even in his mug shot. I printed it and taped it up on my wall. My feelings for him surged all over again. He was a literary James Bond and I, a gay immigrant smuggler. Who knew what we could accomplish if we joined forces! Oliver turning out to be a rare book thief attracted me even more. Perhaps this was part of my problem with men. The badder the bad boy, the worse I wanted him.

"Maybe he *is* perfect for you," Emir said when he came home and I waved the mug shot in his face like a victory flag.

On my lunch break, I sat in my parked car in the agency garage and dialed the detective listed on the website. I wasn't going to turn him in, I told myself. I just needed more information, more details. If I couldn't have Oliver, I would write a story about him, maybe an entire movie. I rationalized the phone call by telling myself I was doing it in the name of research rather than a blend of perverse curiosity and continued Oliver-obsession.

The receptionist at Art Theft said the detective was out. What was this regarding?

"I'm calling to ask a few questions about Oliver Fox," I said.

"Name and phone number, please?"

Uh-oh. Of course she would ask. As Emir and I had been with my mother's visit, I was unprepared. Not having thought of a pseudonym, I panicked.

"Emir al-Habibi!" I blurted.

*REALLY?*

This was the only way my head could think to cover my tracks? I had meant to give a fake name but my synapses misfired and the name of the person I was thinking of burst from my lips—which if I'd looked in the rearview mirror I might have seen turn from pink to white. And then I felt I had no choice but to give her our home phone number.

If the detective reached our answering machine, he would hear Emir's voice saying, *You've reached Emir and Liza.* It could be taken care of easily. I'd get my information about Oliver and that would be the end of it.

Except that's exactly what happened and Emir checked the home messages from his cell phone. I didn't even know we could do that.

"How could you do this to me?" he yelled when he reached me on my phone. "Do you have any idea what a panic attack I had when a detective from the LAPD called for me? This is Detective So-and-So calling for Emir al-Habibi. Are you kidding? I thought your mother decided to have me arrested or we got caught!"

"Em, I am so, so sorry. I was going to tell you . . ."

"I called Omar's lawyer. She said immigration doesn't work through police departments, so I called the detective back and when he said the 'Emira Habibi' who called was a woman, I put two and two together."

"I'm a terrible wife. I'm so sorry."

"Were you trying to turn him in or something?"

"I was trying to . . . find out more about him."

"Well, I have the information for you," Emir said, putting on a sarcasm-soaked secretary voice. "It turned out your book thief already did his time. Though the detective did say he was happy to hear that Oliver was doing well. One of his favorite cases, apparently."

Emir was furious and I felt awful. I'd exploited him. His biggest scare in this process so far and it was all because of me, the one who was supposed to protect him. Instead I had used his name when calling the cops. How could he ever trust me again after such a transgression? Between the aborted road trip and this, I made an even worse wife than I thought I would be.

"Of all the names," Emir said. "Of all the names."

"It's just that I was *thinking* about you."

"Or that you weren't thinking."

"That's exactly what my mother would say."

"I should have known that any girl crazy enough to risk this marriage is crazy in other ways."

"We've been best friends for three years! You know me!"

"You think you know someone and they use your name to call the LAPD to play detective on their book-thief boyfriend."

I had disappointed him. Dismayed in the back office, I kept my eyes on the floor as I rolled my mail cart past Oliver, who had no idea he was the eye of my storm.

Problem: I was terrible at keeping secrets. I showed the Oliver LAPD page to a coworker. By the end of the workday, the entire office was gossiping about it. I hoped no one would trace the rumors back to their original source. *That guy? Really?* people said. Oliver tried to deny the page was real. His defense was that a friend put it up as a joke, but I knew the truth; I had called the detective. If the point of origin was drawn back to me, Oliver would surely retaliate, and the entire office would find out I was married to my Middle Eastern gay friend for his green card. Someone might call the INS on us. This would be the hardest part to tell Emir, that this situation played out exactly as he feared it would.

When I got home from work he was already back from selling spa packages and sat at his desk working on his script. I dropped my bag on the floor and kicked off my shoes.

"You're not going to like this," I said.

"What happened this time?"

I told him about the leak. He launched into his *I knew it-* and-*I told you so's*. I did not argue or try to explain. There was nothing I could say. Emir had predicted a negative outcome in the Oliver situation, even though he could not have known the extent of it.

We turned frustration into action and put a plan in place. At work the next day, no one seemed to know I was the one who outed Oliver as the rare book thief, but I gave my notice anyway. Dorothy wished me well. I didn't say good-bye to Oliver.

I had wanted to be a hero to Emir, but I was no hero. I'd always lost my head in love, would go to any length to get what I wanted. It happened again with Oliver, but what I was really in over my head with was my unconventional marriage. I'd thought life could go on as it had before, but I couldn't continue to do as I pleased. I had married into a high-stakes situation and it was time to become more of the adult I thought I wanted to be. Desiring to grow up fast—the *idea* of adulthood, commitment, and settling down—and its actualities were quite different things. Marriage is partnership, and even though Emir was a partner of a different nature, this definition stood nonetheless. Having sold out my partner for selfish reasons showed me that thinking this marriage would be easy and seamless had been a mistake. It was a huge responsibility. My intentions and the reality of the situation wouldn't always align, and, if this was going to work, I had to become more sensitive to my husband's needs.

## 10.

## The Great Escape

"We can't impose our definition of marriage, especially being in New York. We've seen it all."
—Maria Guerra,
United States Citizenship and Immigration Services

We left no forwarding address. On a cold, blustery April morning in 2002, five months later than we had originally planned, Emir and I arrived at Forty West 22nd Street in Manhattan. It often happens that we are right about where our paths will lead, we just go about getting there by a different means than originally planned. Uncle Vance, my grandfather's brother, offered to let Emir and me stay in his loft, where we would sleep in the same wall-less open space where he brought folding chairs for the audience to sit on performance days. Two twin beds were pushed up against opposite walls. During the day our beds were covered in fake leather, disguised as couches. The steam heater rattled all night.

We didn't tell Uncle Vance that we were married—no point in forcing him to choose loyalty to me or to his niece, my mother, even though the bumper stickers on his door clearly announced his causes: Human Rights Campaign, LAMBDA, ACLU, Amnesty International, GLAAD, PFLAG, Stonewall Democrats. As a gay rights activist whose own mother sent him to a psychiatrist to "cure" him, Uncle Vance would likely have been supportive, but he was also close with my mother. So *why chance it* won out, especially after the Oliver situation.

"Hello, hello, hello!" Uncle Vance shouted, ambling down the hallway to meet us by the elevator, which opened straight into the loft. "Welcome welcome welcome! Oh my my *my*, would you look at all these suitcases suitcases *suitcases!*"

We had five suitcases between us and glanced at each other, having the same thought about the twenty-five-box shipment arriving the day after tomorrow.

I hugged Uncle Vance and stepped aside to introduce him to Emir. After greetings and welcomes, Emir and I retreated to the theater space to put our things away, behind curtains concealing an area for wardrobe, props, and quick costume changes. There were drawers of uniformly blue prop furniture and rolling wardrobe racks. Everything here was movable, stand-in, temporary. The unconscious seeks outward manifestation, and though I hadn't designed this space, it seemed fitting that this was where I landed.

That was childhood: a series of places, different identities tried on like costumes pulled from one of these wardrobe racks, or scenes from Uncle Ridgebert's magic carpet ride.

During my childhood visits to the loft, Vance's partner, Uncle Ridgebert, brought me into the space, spread a rug—a traditional rug from Emiristan, actually—on the creaky hardwood floor, dimmed the bright white spotlights and turned on the colorful ones. I knew we were embarking on my favorite journey of all: an imaginary one—a magic carpet ride. He held a string of bells that reminded me of a Santa Claus sleigh; he shook them every time we passed into new territory, and then described the beautiful scenes, adapted from his own travels with Vance. From Ridgebert's words, pronounced in his slow Texan drawl, I could picture the places passing below: the lights of Paris, the smell of spices in Tangier marketplaces, morning prayers sung from the Blue Mosque in Istanbul, car horns and traffic passing by below the great pyramids of Cairo, the Piraeus port in Athens, ferries departing for the islands. Though I traveled to these places with my mother, Ridge made them feel more entrancing somehow. When he died, I was halfway across the world in Rome, attending middle school. It felt as if it didn't really happen—as if he had hopped on his magic carpet and flown away.

After that, Uncle Vance created a show called *Gilbert Without Sullivan*.

A one-man show.

A flair for the theatrical ran in the family.

Vance and Ridgebert had put on countless Gilbert and Sullivan musicals over the years, and were fond of saying that G & S, like V & R, brought separate and equally important skills to the table. Ridge even resembled Sullivan, while Vance fit the

Gilbert mold. My great-uncles were a study in opposites, better together because they each brought to the relationship—both professionally and personally—qualities the other lacked. They were each other's greatest champions. Ridge was sweet, gentle, and slow-moving, while Vance was spitfire-quick in gesture and wit. Ridge cooked gourmet meals; Vance sipped gin and tonics at the table and talked a blue streak about his new play or book about his methods of coaching actors. They studied with Lee Strasberg and Stella Adler, and they didn't want to have children but had a large and extended makeshift family of students and friends who were in and out at odd hours.

When Ridgebert died, Vance said he lost a part of himself. He talked about Ridge all the time—productions they had worked on together, their travels, Ridge's birthday. I idealized Vance and Ridgebert's relationship—they were the only couple in my immediate family purview who did not divorce—and they couldn't even get married.

The next morning, we sat at the breakfast table poring over apartment listings while Uncle Vance gave private acting classes in our makeshift bedroom. Mohammad had offered to help with any deposits we couldn't afford and I was grateful for the father-in-law who was, financially, the kind of father I'd always wondered what it would be like to have. I felt guilty about accepting help but I would also never turn it down when it was needed.

Under a pile of newspapers, I came across a December 2001 issue of *The New Yorker*, its cover portraying New York City's neighborhoods with satirical Middle-Eastern sounding names ("Khandibar," "Flatbushtuns," "Fugged-abouditstan"). I pointed out Chelsea on the map, laughing:

"Look! Gaymenistan! *Gaymenistan!*" I thought it was so clever, and laughed and laughed before realizing that Emir had not joined in. "What's the matter? You don't think it's hilarious?"

"No. It's not," he said, his voice flat. He gaped at me as if I'd just said the earth was, too.

"How do you not find this comical?"

"That," he pointed at the offending cover as if it were a rat I'd picked up by the tail, "is in poor taste. Inappropriate, insensitive, and quite offensive, actually."

I disagreed about the cover. He was misinterpreting the humor, taking the cartoon map too seriously. Then he spelled out what the cover brought up for him. He thought it was a symbol of a world turned hateful, and he was of two groups on the receiving end.

"In the Middle East I'm an unwanted gay person, and in America an unwanted Arab," he said. "So tell me, where should I go?"

What we needed was a place where every misfit fit in.

On the F train bound for the East Village, passengers slept, read, or stared into space. For us, the subway was still an adventure. *Why weren't all these people excited to be here, too?* We hadn't yet acquired New York City jadedness. The rest of the ride was spent inventing backstories for the other commuters, whispered in each other's ears all the way to the 2nd Avenue station.

There were several two-bedroom apartments listed under the East Village column in the paper, and we called a broker who would meet us on the corner of 7th Street and Avenue A. Emir and I shared a bowl of steamed vegetables and brown rice with carrot-ginger dressing at 7A. We sat on the sidewalk patio even though a chilly wind blew, discussing whether or not to tell the broker that we were married. Might it give us an advantage in the competitive below-14th-Street apartment market? It couldn't hurt. Even seven months after September 11th and four since the anthrax scares, the Manhattan apartment hunt was competitive.

The broker found us on the corner and introduced herself. She was in her forties and had a nasal voice reminiscent of Fran Drescher from the 1990s sitcom *The Nanny*, long dark hair, and a bow-lipped, red-tinted smile. Running shoes bottomed off her pinstriped suit; black heels poked out of her purse. The woman meant business.

"I'm Emir al-Habibi and this is my wife, Liza," Emir said.

"No way," said Fran. "How old are you guys?"

"Twenty-two," I said. "We were married by an Elvis impersonator in Las Vegas this past November."

Fran laughed. "So what do you need the second bedroom for?"

"An office!" (Me.) "A baby!" (Him.)

"I see," said Fran.

She looked from me to Emir and back again. I didn't want to imagine how we might contradict each other during the INS interview. We had to get our spiel more ironclad than this. Then again, what married couple didn't contradict each other when telling their stories?

The undercurrent of paranoia that ran beneath this whole endeavor surfaced then. That we were playing with fire, that showing up at the INS having married such an obviously gay man would be seen as nothing more than a silly farce. Fran had brought up precisely what I feared: that we looked exactly as I thought we did, that we hadn't fooled anyone, that we never could.

I didn't say this aloud but I could tell Emir felt it, too. It hovered between us: the unspoken, The Lack.

Apartment after apartment blurred into one collective image of a dump. There was the one on 13th Street and Avenue B where you had to shimmy through a narrow gap between two poorly constructed false walls to get into the kitchen. And the one on Sullivan Street with the toilet in a padlocked closet down the hall, its bathtub adjacent to the refrigerator. I'd thought those were urban legend. There was the place east of Tompkins Square Park where the warped floor undulated like ocean waves, as if giants were curled up asleep underneath it. There was a pair of bunk beds in every room.

Emir shook his head. Fran asked if we'd considered Staten Island. I loved islands. Islands evoked tranquility and ease, feelings I did not often experience.

"I've heard there's a nice nature preserve there," I said.

Emir looked at me with an expression of horror.

"Okay, no Staten."

There was one apartment left. The three of us walked to another tenement (I'd lost track as to how many we'd visited that day) and ascended six flights of stairs. Emir was out of breath as we reached the highest landing.

"You'll have to quit smoking if we live here," I said.

"If it's a good apartment, hand to God I will." He shot me his fake smile.

Fran jingled through her massive keychain, trying several keys before she found the right one. She pushed open the apartment door and stepped aside for us to enter. Clean, shiny hardwood floors. Windows, large windows, three exposures. A view almost all the way to the Hudson to the west, the Williamsburg and Manhattan bridges to the south, and the Empire State Building to the north. We made our way through the space as if we'd drifted into a dream. Other than the stairs it was perfect and in our price range, though barely, at seventeen hundred dollars a month.

"Why is it less than those other, worse apartments?" I whispered to Emir. "Something's gotta be wrong with it."

We opened cupboards and closets, turned on faucets, checked the water pressure. We searched and searched for hidden flaws and all we could turn up was that one of the bedrooms did not have a closet, which was not really a problem—I could bring over one of the rolling wardrobe racks from the loft. Emir told Fran we loved it. We would take it.

Fran said she would run our credit checks and get back to us.

After saying good-bye to Fran, Emir and I rode all the way to Coney Island. A frigid wind tainted the end of April, but we ran over the empty boardwalk and down to the beach anyway, first picking up Corona beer and fried frog legs at the one snack shack that was open. We kicked off our shoes and sat on the sand, the Ferris wheel a dark skeleton against the first horizon we'd seen since leaving Los Angeles. I nestled my cheek against the fake fur of Emir's jacket collar and he kissed the top of my head. We fell into a comfortable silence and stayed that way for a while. I felt strangely nostalgic for the present, thinking of how it would feel to remember it. I ran sand through my fingers, letting some fall into my shoes.

When I finished my beer, I stashed the bottle into my purse when Emir wasn't looking. Later, back at the loft, Uncle Vance's intern asked what the heck I was doing when he caught me standing over the kitchen sink, shaking my shoe over a plastic green funnel implanted in an empty Corona.

"Just trying to save something," I said.

"All right, but don't let Vance see you putting dirt in the sink."

I kept looping around the same mental track: if our marriage was not really a marriage, then how to explain the need I felt for Emir? Was it that we completed each other? Was it less valid because it was not sexual, or was it up to us to decide what makes a marriage for ourselves? I wished away the social and legal aspects of marriage and denied the contradictions and complications in hopes that we could redefine it for ourselves, that we had created a niche form of a union.

Emir and I would return to Coney Island for the Mermaid Parade that summer, but with the crowds and chaos and noise it wasn't as good as that first sojourn, when we sat at the edge of the City. Waves collapsed on the sand like weary lovers, seagulls shrilled and dove into the sea. In that moment, it felt as if nothing mattered—not The Big Mom in the Sky, not apartment obstacles, not the immigration quest, not the instability of our lives. In the off-season emptiness of pure space, the beach was all ours and it felt as if nothing could stand in our way.

The apartment on the Lower East Side was ours—almost.

When we arrived at the broker's Midtown office, Fran's boss, a handsome British man, told us he had prepared the formal application and paperwork, but our financials and employment history were lacking. Emir and I were twenty-three and twenty-two years old, and we couldn't compete with the young i-bankers and first-year associates who wanted the same apartments. We fancied ourselves self-sufficient adults but the need for a guarantor reminded us that we were fledglings, still tethered to parental sheetrock. (Or Emir was; I stubbornly scraped by, insisting on the financial independence I knew would make my mother proud.) Mohammad had offered to help; we were once again going to take him up on it.

Emir called Mohammad, who, without question or protest, agreed to sign for us. It was so easy! I wished that I could ask my mother for help the way Emir could ask Mohammad—and Mohammad would give his son what he asked for with pleasure. Why else did he earn all that money, if not to help his children? It's an awkward subject, asking for help from parents. At some point you come across as spoiled and entitled. In some ways that's exactly what I was, given my upbringing. Though we weren't rich I was raised around the wealthy—the children of powerful people who ran Mexico. I went to their schools, ate in their restaurants. Since the government paid our rent and expenses, my mother could afford for us to travel. It was the kind of lifestyle that bred the idea I could do and become anything, that if I set goals and went about achieving them, it would all work out. Were Emir and I just two self-entitled people in our twenties who thought we should be allowed whatever we wanted, whether staying in America or an apartment in the East Village?

Quite possibly this was true about us. Being nice people didn't mean we weren't spoiled. As much as I felt guilty, turning down Mohammad's help was not an option. What I was going to do was get on the phone and thank my father-in-law for his generosity. He was gracious. His deep voice on the other end of the line said it was his pleasure and he looked forward to meeting me the next time he came to New York on business. When was that going to be? I wanted to know. Sometime in the next few months, he said. After we were settled in he was going to organize a business trip around visiting us. Part of me wanted to tell him not to but the other, larger part wanted to meet the man who made Emir, and the contradictions Mohammad embodied—the homophobe who was kind at heart. How those negative qualities in him did not undercut his kindness. I wondered how someone could be hateful because of concepts and ideals, but generous and loving on the personal level, and how that would change if Mohammad knew his son preferred his intimate relationships to be with men, not with me.

The broker prepared the paperwork. There was a line asking for the guarantor's Social Security number, which Emir left blank. When he handed the form back, the broker tapped on the sheet where the missing numbers should go, as if it was an oversight.

"You need to include his Social Security number," he said.

"He doesn't have one," said Emir.

"Is your father a U.S. citizen or resident?" the broker asked.

"No, but I knew plenty of international students who rented apartments when I was in college; their parents weren't citizens or residents . . . how do international students at NYU or Columbia rent off-campus apartments?"

"There are buildings that do that. This isn't one of them."

Our guarantor had to have a U.S. Social Security number, one of the few things Mohammad didn't have.

"We're going to have to ask your mother," Emir said.

"Please, no."

"What about Uncle Vance?"

I shook my head. "He doesn't make any money."

"So we don't have a choice other than going back to the listings."

"She is going to hate this."

I dialed my mother's cell phone number. She was sitting on a donkey in a crevasse on the island of Crete. The connection was bad, full of static and feedback. I explained that the situation was a simple matter of signing a form, and that she would never have to pay our rent. I said it all in one breathless sentence.

"But if I'm your guarantor," she said, "I would be responsible for *Emir's* rent."

"If anything went wrong on Emir's end, Mohammad would send him money," I said. "You wouldn't have to do a thing."

"I won't take on legal responsibility for *Emir*," she said.

I knew she wasn't into doing favors. *If only you knew how legally responsible I am for Emir,* I thought.

"No one will rent us an apartment without a guarantor," I protested. "We didn't know about this Social Security number glitch. Mohammad was more than willing, why aren't you?"

"I don't feel comfortable taking on this kind of financial responsibility when it isn't only you I'm responsible for," she said. "Plus I told you not to move there."

I remembered exactly what she said: *The city isn't safe. There's anthrax. The whole place is a mess.* I had disobeyed. Was she trying to teach me a lesson?

"But I'm already here."

Emir reached his hand out for the phone.

"Let me talk to her," he said.

I handed over the telephone. The broker gave us a puzzled look—*what's wrong with these people?*

"Penny? Hi, it's me, Emir. I wanted to tell you that I will always pay my share of rent. I am really responsible. I've never paid even a phone bill late, much less a credit card bill, and I would never, ever put you in that position. If I don't find a job and I run out of money, my dad will cover me. My father has his own business so money won't be a problem. . . . No, Penny, she doesn't waste money. . . . Yes, she is very responsible."

He rolled his eyes at me as if to say *your mother thinks you're a little kid.* Long pause. I paced back and forth.

"But I am. No, we *are.* All right. Mmm-hmm. Yes. I understand," he said. I stared at Emir, pleading with my eyes for more of a sign as to how it was going. Pause. "Okay. Do you want to speak to her again? Okay. All right. 'Bye."

Emir placed the broker's phone back on the receiver.

"Penny says no."

My stomach dropped. Why wouldn't she back me up, take care of me? All we needed was a signature on a dotted line.

The British broker said he was sorry, but unless we could

show that we would be earning enough to make rent, we would need a guarantor.

Emir and I walked from the broker's office in Midtown through the tourist bustle and Disneyland charm of Times Square and all the way back to the loft feeling defeated but optimistic; we could extend our search to Brooklyn and Queens—"Fran mentioned Staten Island . . ." I said, to Emir's chagrin—or stay in the loft until we found jobs. We weren't lawyers or investment bankers. With our film degrees and no other experience, no one was going to hire us for that high of a starting salary, but since we were married, both our incomes would be considered as one. The search would simply need to shift: first jobs, then apartment. We were disappointed, but it wasn't like we were going to be out on the street. We could rent a storage space for our boxes and keep looking. Still, the unknown was nervous-making.

"One day we will look back at this and laugh," Emir said. "We'll say, 'Remember when we couldn't even rent an apartment?'"

I smiled, feeling a little bit better outside in the cool air, walking down Sixth Avenue with Emir by my side. "One day we'll say, 'Uncle Em and Mommy will always be your guarantors.'"

"Or 'Auntie Liza and Daddy will.'"

"Either way."

"Or both."

"Probably both."

Back at the loft, Emir put a Liza Minnelli record on Uncle Vance's old player. We sang loudly along with my namesake, begging New York to come through for us. Then I tossed a salad, Emir sliced crudités for a hummus platter, and Uncle Vance prepared gazpacho, pasta, and vegetables. We told him about apartment hunting and our failure to secure one. It wasn't that my mother didn't want to help me or that she had something to prove by turning down the role of guarantor, Uncle Vance said. From so far away, it was difficult for my mother to be clear on what we were doing and how; from far away, she couldn't tell that I had grown up at all. I was frozen in her mind as the seventeen-year-old she left in a college dorm on move-in day.

We sat down to eat. As Emir and I went back and forth explaining the intricacies of renting an apartment in New York City, Vance had an idea. Emir and I needed to earn a combined fifty-six thousand dollars a year; what if he typed up letters of employment on Masterworks Laboratory Theater letterhead stating that we were new hires—as managers of marketing and publicity—for thirty thousand dollars per year each.

"They won't ask you for *our* financials," he said. "If only we could hire publicists! Yes, yes, what a good story to get you the apartment, *The Apartment*! Have you seen that movie? A classic, classic, *classic.*"

"I love that movie," Emir said.

We agreed to go back to the broker and try it, if the apartment was still available. If not, armed with our fake employment letters Uncle Vance typed up on his IBM Selectric, at least we could resume the search.

My mother called back in the morning.

Refusing to be our guarantor was harsh and untrusting, and

would I accept her apology? I told her we already had the place, that Vance helped us out and we were moving in the following day.

"What did Vance do to help?" she asked suspiciously.

I told her he had written us fake letters of employment.

"It's not right of him to do that."

"He's probably as eager for Emir and me to have our own place as we are."

"Deceit is not the way to go about it."

We signed the lease with my mother's name attached as our guarantor, and rerouted the shipment of belongings to our new address. Emir and I took the free bus from Port Authority to the Ikea in Elizabeth, New Jersey like any other newlywed couple in the Tri-State Area. I remembered my mother's rescue efforts in L.A., building Ikea furniture as a consolation strategy for the ended engagement, an attempt to heal through unrelated action, through focus on a concrete task. She said it was the best way. Stay active, move on. In our tiny living room, planks and sticks became bookshelves and drawers, things we could look at, pieces that came together to form recognizable objects.

# 11.
## The Science of Arrangement

Our apartment was strewn with boxes. No matter how many times I moved, it was still overwhelming. I pulled out the AbFab poster that read sin is in, sweetie! and the nobody knows i'm gay magnet. The picture of us on the Stratosphere in Las Vegas. My various mementos from travels over the years, even an old airplane bottle of Spanish wine. Magnets of the row houses on Amsterdam's canals. I gazed upon these objects as though they were old friends. I wanted to get rid of things but it never seemed to happen. I was a bona fide pack rat, a hoarder of memories.

We sat on the floor opening boxes and stayed up all night unpacking until the new apartment resembled our old one, only a lot smaller. I put the beer bottle with Coney Island sand up on my bookshelf next to a wedding photo of us dancing in front of Elvis. Emir strictly prohibited my putting that *New Yorker* cover on the refrigerator with the nobody knows i'm gay magnet.

Lilah referred us to the man who was to become our New York City lawyer. We went to his office in the Financial District for our first meeting, a simple matter of going through our files, discussing timelines (the interview was not likely to happen anytime soon, given the post–September 11th backlog), and to catch him up on our story. The new lawyer was a white man in his sixties with thick gray hair and small glasses he kept pushing up the bridge of his nose. His paralegal was a young woman in her thirties with straight black hair and a red skirt suit.

"How are you doing today?" she asked Emir and me with a wide, whitened smile.

"I'm having such a bad hair day," Emir said, as if it was the most natural, normal thing to say in your immigration lawyer's office when you were trying to pretend to be someone you weren't. I kicked him under the table. "But other than that I'm great!"

After forty minutes of paper shuffling, we walked back out onto lower Broadway.

"Do you think they became suspicious because of my comment?" he asked.

"I think you have a good excuse," I said.

"What do you mean?"

"You're foreign," I said. "In Emiristan it might be a typical greeting to talk about hair. If you ever slip, chalk it up to a cultural difference."

There might be some overlap, I thought, between perceptions of foreign and gay. The boys I went to high school with in Mexico City dressed impeccably, gelled their hair, and groomed like peacocks. They were as into their appearance as the girls.

Emir could use his foreignness as an excuse. The so-called Eurotrash guys who cruised up and down Newbury Street in their Ferraris when we were in college wore cashmere scarves and Prada loafers. Just like Emir.

"Or I can just practice not talking about bad hair days to lawyers."

"Or that."

I lifted my arm to hail a cab.

After a year of silence, an email from Julian arrived in my inbox. My breath caught in my throat when I saw his name in bold amongst ads for penis enlargement and a forward from my grandmother that surely contained captioned photographs of cats. The content of the email was even more shocking than its arrival: Julian broke his leg while swimming in the ocean in Mexico, on vacation with his then-girlfriend, another investment banker. A blood clot had formed, dislodged, and caught in one of his lungs. The doctors thought he was going to die. In the hospital, he wrote, he thought of me.

Against all odds, he survived. Again.

I thought of how Julian was nothing if not a survivor. Born three months premature, doctors said he would die then, too. Instead, he survived every day inside an incubator. When he was ten, he fell three stories over a balcony in Mexico City, landing on his head. He was medevac-ed to Texas in a coma, where doctors said he would die. He didn't. The Coca-Cola baby, he called himself, because when he was born he weighed the same as a two-liter Coke bottle, would not be taken out. He was born a fighter.

The person I loved since the age of sixteen—quite possibly the only man I loved despite having been with many—had been on the third so-called deathbed of his young life and thought of me. All the old feelings rushed back.

Julian was living on a floor of a brownstone in Park Slope, and I went to see him. He had two cats. They had knocked over the overflowing trash can in the kitchen. Keeping up with his demanding career while he was injured left him little time for household maintenance. We went into his bedroom. There was a photograph of Julian with the Acapulco-accident ex-girl-friend, a pretty Indian thirtysomething, on a high shelf. I asked him to take it down so I could look at it.

"Why did you guys break up?" I asked.

He shrugged. "We didn't get along anymore."

It would be a long time yet before I found out the truth about what happened with them. That would come the same night I found out the truth about us. But right then it all felt blissful. I could hardly believe it was Julian, he was here, this was real again. The same familiar cologne he'd worn since college was bitter on my tongue as I kissed his neck, inhaling deeply. His skin felt so familiar against mine.

"You still have the tattoo," he said, running his thumb over it.

"You don't," I noticed.

It had been covered up with something resembling a large black blob.

"I didn't think we would ever get back together. I was

trying to break with the past. And she didn't like me having it."

"Okay," I said, not caring because I was so happy to be in his arms again.

We lay in his big bed together afterward. I was sure this was it: we were back together and I'd stocked up enough good karma that this time it would work. We would get re-engaged, I would move into this beautiful, empty brownstone and Julian and I would have our happily-ever-after. To do so, I had to be completely honest, though. I had to tell him about Emir. I hoped he would understand. I'd been saying for a long time that the right man for me would get it. He would be supportive and see the marriage as I did, as a generous, significant act performed for one of the most important people in my life, a friend so close I thought of him as family, the brother I never had.

Curled up in the blankets, I told Julian there was something he needed to know.

"I'm kind of married," I offered, taking secret delight in his confounded expression before I added, "but don't worry. I married Emir."

Instead of the relieved chuckle and immediate understanding I had half-hoped for, half-expected, Julian was furious.

"What? How could you?"

He got out of bed and started putting on his clothes with his back to me. I sat up, pulling the blankets tight around my body.

"I did it for his green card," I explained, "because otherwise he was going to have to go back to Emiristan right after September eleventh."

"Yeah, I figured that was the reason. You know that's totally illegal, right? You of all people . . . how could you not know better?"

"I wanted to help him. You and I broke up . . ."

"So you go and marry a gay guy? Why should Emir get a free pass? I've been working my ass off in this country for years and I don't have a green card. What does Emir even do?"

"He's a screenwriter," I said.

"He's a freeloader."

"That's not fair. You don't even know him."

"I've had to stress out over keeping my H-1B every year, constantly dealing with incompetent immigration lawyers who screw up my paperwork and all this bureaucracy, and you *gave* him this thing—"

"I didn't give it to him for no reason."

"This incredible privilege he didn't *do* anything to *earn!*"

I felt like a little kid being yelled at by her dad—the first time I had ever experienced that feeling. My father had never yelled at me. He wasn't around enough to have assumed any sort of disciplinary role.

"Are you still married?" Julian asked.

"Yes."

I almost said I was sorry. Instead, I got up and got dressed, too.

"Green card marriage is cheating. I can't believe you would . . . does Penny know?"

"No."

"You know she's going to find out, right?"

"She won't."

I suddenly felt even smaller than I was.

"Are you kidding me? Of *course* she will, if she hasn't already."

"She really hasn't. There's no way she could know and keep quiet about it. And anyway, this isn't about my mother."

"It's totally about your mother. This is *all* about your mother."

I didn't know how to explain to him that it was more than that, that the friendship Emir and I shared was so important to me I had done it based on my own need, too. I didn't want to argue. Julian had gone against my fundamental rule for dating, that any man who would be the right partner for me would understand my bond with Emir and the reasons why I married him. But since he was Julian, and he predated my rule, I did not consider this.

Julian's next email arrived on Monday. It stated he couldn't see me, that we should leave things be. He needed to focus entirely on his job and I would distract him. I knew the real reason. There could be no going back, this time it was really over. It was a repeat of December 2000. I cried and Emir rushed to comfort me. This time, there were no love letters to burn over a drain.

A few days later, it was my turn to rush to comfort him: Emir had his own romantic trauma. I came home to find him smoking and crying on the fire escape outside the kitchen window.

"What happened?" I asked, crawling out to join him.

"Carey. I ran into Carey in Tompkins Square Park."

Carey. Emir's first love, the first man who broke his heart.

"And it didn't go well," I said.

Emir shook his head. "No, it did. It went very well."

"Now I'm confused."

"I was walking through the park when I heard, 'Emir?' behind me. I turned around and it was him. He looked great. Except he lost too much weight."

He wiped his eyes and took a drag off the cigarette. I took it from him, pulled on it, and handed it back. Emir went on.

"He invited me for coffee. I was so excited. Some part of me holds onto the idea that he's my soul mate. We had a wonderful time in the café. We still finish each other's sentences. I knew how easily I could love him again, and it seemed like he could love me again, too."

"But he has a boyfriend?"

Tears welled in Emir's eyes again.

"We both wanted to see each other again as soon as possible, like for a real date. He invited me to dinner but he said he couldn't do it until the week after next because he is *studying for the exam to be an INS officer.*"

"Holy crap."

"It makes sense, with his background . . ."

Carey spoke five languages.

Emir started to cry again.

"You didn't—"

"No, I hadn't told him. I was about to before he said that."

"Well, it's Carey . . . he wouldn't do anything."

"He said as soon as he takes the test his schedule will free up and he would love to spend time with me. Why, God, why?"

"Why can't you? Just don't tell him!"

"I can't take that chance," Emir said. "I can't."

There were ghosts everywhere and they were haunting us. I thought our marriage would keep us from the wrong men.

Since both of us seemed to choose the wrong men, maybe it was already working. What I hadn't considered was that we could actually get hurt. Maybe by keeping us from Julian and Carey, it was protecting us from worse pain. We couldn't know for sure. The marriage may have been a litmus test, but it was no magic shield. What if Carey *was* the one? What if I had ruined Emir's big chance at true love? Then I remembered he wouldn't have been here to have it, that in Emiristan his chances at love would take place in back alleys and secret meeting points. Those chances at love could end in violence, hate crimes, death. It was hard to remember the big stakes and risks as we were living our little daily lives, running around the city and into ex-boyfriends and fiancés, trying to find our place, trying to find our way.

"The right man for you wouldn't be an INS officer anyway," I said. "He's more of a creative type, and he's out there somewhere, walking the earth right now, and one day you'll meet."

"I hope so," Emir said, stubbing out the cigarette and slipping through the window into the kitchen. I followed my husband back inside our home.

Soon we had an East Village nightlife routine, a breadcrumb path we followed faithfully around the neighborhood. Starlight Lounge on Avenue A and Eleventh replaced the Abbey. After that we headed to the Phoenix, and at the end of the night, the infamous Cock. It has since moved and cleaned up, but in 2002 it was notorious for its back room, where one could sample the merchandise before deciding what to take home. We would wander around meeting people, having random conversations, and hoping each night would be the one that led to some great and memorable adventure—or, for Emir, a boyfriend. I knew I wasn't going to meet anyone for me, not in that scene, but it was the first time I was not looking, so I didn't care.

What I was looking for was work, and since having worked in a talent agency mailroom apparently qualified me to work in another talent agency mailroom, I was called for an interview at the William Morris Agency, for a position in their historic agent trainee program. Agent trainees began in the mailroom and, once they learned the ropes, had a chance at being hired to work as agent's assistants in specific departments: Television Talent, Television Literary, Motion Picture Talent, Motion Picture Literary, Corporate Consulting, Lectures, Books, Music, and Theater. Before the interview, I had already decided the book department was where I wanted to land. New York being the center of the publishing industry was rekindling my often-snuffed dream of becoming a writer. I pushed the dream aside because it was impractical, because no one *really* made a living as a writer, it was a hobby to be done on the side. Real work, work you were paid to do, wasn't supposed to be the thing you loved doing most. I was beginning to realize that there were writers who made their passion into their career, and that these writers had literary agents. If I worked for a literary agent, I could learn how actual writers made money writing.

The initial interview process happened in two rounds: a typing and grammar test, and since I passed that, a meeting with Human Resources. I passed the second stage, and so I made it to the third and final round—an interview in which I would sit at the head of a conference table surrounded by eight agents, four on each side: little twenty-two-year-old me and eight of the most powerful agents in New York City's entertainment and media industries. It was intimidating and I was suddenly grateful for my mother dragging me to all those diplomatic parties where I learned how to talk to adults.

The morning of the interview, I dressed in a charcoal gray pantsuit that said "I am a serious businessperson in the making" and a pink button-down shirt that said "but not too proud to be your girlish secretary." The panel interview was fantastic practice for the INS because I had to pretend. I talked about why I wanted to be a literary agent, about shepherding authors through the publishing process and why that was my career goal. It wasn't, and I was really interviewing to spy on the literary department, undercover and in disguise, so that I could figure out how to *be* a client, not how to represent them. I don't remember how I convinced the agents, but they were all smiling and nodding. Two days later I got the call from Human Resources that I was hired and should report to the mailroom on Monday.

The mailroom job paid four hundred and fifty dollars a week. On our first day, the other new hires and I received little charts of who was who and who sat where, and the head trainee highlighted the mail routes in pink, green, yellow, and blue. The agency occupied the 15th and 16th floors of the Midtown skyscraper. The mailroom was in the basement. We took the freight elevator up (the 4 PM mail run was the worst because we had to ride up with the garbage) and were responsible for one of four runs: 15A, 15B, 16A, or 16B. We traded off the runs, with two trainees getting to sit each one out as there were six of us in total. No one ever wanted 16A because it was the longest route, around the television department and all the way through Books.

We trainees were a motley crew, *The Breakfast Club* in suits. The head trainee, Sultan, was a former investment banker. The other new hires were Patrick, a good-looking and well-groomed Connecticut WASP; Vinny, a rebel who was a political hire, the son of someone's client's best friend; and Brad, a very liberal nice Jewish boy from L.A. (the kind of boy my mother would have liked me to date) who ate seaweed every day for lunch. We were soon joined by Carolyn, a thirty-year-old, Oxford-educated genius who was raised in elite Hollywood circles; and Ralphie, whose father was a famous novelist, and who had a penchant for greeting us with a loud, enthusiastic, "WHASSUP NIGGAAAZZZ!?" in spite of the fact that he was white and born and raised on the Upper West Side. We all rolled our eyes at Ralphie. Sultan barked at him to sit his ass down and get to work slicing up the newspapers for Clippings, the daily agency briefing of relevant entertainment stories that trainees were responsible for compiling. We sliced up *The New York Times, The Wall Street Journal, New York Post, Daily News,* and, on Wednesdays, the *Village Voice.* On days we were assigned to do Clippings, we had to arrive at the office by 7:30 AM. So much for my New York nightlife, but it wouldn't exactly be a bad thing to start going to bed earlier, at a decent human hour like the rest of the working world. I was grateful to be among them.

During Clippings, Patrick and Brad would really get into it. Patrick was a Republican, and Brad, the ultraliberal, challenged him on everything. The two of them entered voracious political debates every morning based on the stories in the news, usually about President Bush and the lies he and his cronies told our country (Brad) versus liberals' eagerness to vilify a president who was actually doing a good job (Patrick). Since they were both Ivy League graduates, the debates were cerebral and intense, too much so for me to handle before I'd had my coffee. I put my headphones on and pressed play on my old yellow sports Discman as I sliced away at the newspapers. It was way too early to talk politics.

Nights before the mornings I had Clippings, I did not make the gay bar rounds with Emir. One of those nights, at Starlight, Emir met a new guy. Drew was a fine art dealer and exactly Emir's blond, blue-eyed, baby-faced type. He moved to New York from Cleveland in his late twenties and was thirtysomething now. The first thing I noticed about him was that he must work out obsessively to maintain that kind of physique. He was bulky and muscular and wore a leather cap. My stomach clenched. Something wasn't right but it was only a feeling, an impression.

Drew held down two jobs, the one he called his "respectable" position—art dealer for a well-established Chelsea institution—the other his "money" gig as a freelance paparazzo. Drew was a member of an elite loop informed of the whereabouts of Britney, Lindsay, Angelina, Brad, and Tom; he sold his photographs to the tabloids for enough money to afford a loft in SoHo. This was all I knew about Drew. Drew was a mystery, or at least to me he was, but soon he and Emir were inseparable. I felt as if I was losing Emir and I was; I was losing my husband to another man—I assumed that this was why I didn't like Drew as much as I thought I should. I intuited a mean streak. This was all based on a first impression and a conversation that didn't go much past "hello" and "nice to finally meet you."

I heard in Drew's voice that he was not really happy to meet me, either. All I could tell by the way Emir put both arms around Drew's waist and kissed him on the cheek, and the way Drew lay his palm atop Emir's curls as if he were a pet, was that this was going to be a tangled relationship. There was something about Drew that I didn't trust. I hoped it would be a transitional fling for Emir, to help him forget the run-in with Carey.

Was my hurt genuine or was some part of me faking it so I could feel rejected—the comfortable state I made sure every man I got involved with repeated?

When Emir asked what I thought of Drew, I said I thought he was great, just great.

"Did you know he served in the military?" Emir said.

I shoveled chopsticks into take-out Japanese one weekday evening at home. Emir sat with me, sipping a glass of Coke.

"No, he didn't tell me that."

I felt as if I understood Drew a little better after learning he had a double identity at one point too. It helped explain why he seemed suspicious and closed off.

Still, I didn't resent his presence any less.

"What?" I asked.

Emir was giving me a funny look, his mouth partway open as if to speak words he didn't really want to say, an eyebrow raised.

"Am I neglecting you?" he said.

Here was the chance to have an honest conversation about our expectations, needs, and desires. I didn't want Emir to feel guilty, though, and whenever I met someone I liked as much as he liked Drew, I would want to spend all my time with him, too. I wouldn't want to have to worry about making Emir feel neglected. So instead, I said:

"No, honey, of all people I understand. When you're first in a relationship you want to spend all your time with that person."

"Are you sure? You can tell me if you feel like I'm not paying you enough attention."

"I don't need attention," I lied.

I finished my shu mai and dug chopsticks into sticky rice.

"Want some?" I asked.

"I already ate. Just some leftover pasta. I would have offered to heat you a plate."

"Don't worry about it. I was craving Japanese."

He went back into his room and shut the French doors.

I wasn't in love with Emir, but maybe it was I, not Drew, who wanted his complete devotion. Maybe I didn't dislike Drew because of anything to do with Drew, but because he'd taken the one I'd settled into believing was mine alone—all mine and the only one I had. I was not proud of this. I said I didn't want that kind of control over another person but that's what I signed up for. When I felt I was losing him to another, that this new boyfriend was more important than me, I became a jealous wife. I wanted Emir back. I wanted him for my own. Of course he was going to find a boyfriend again, especially now that we were finally settling down somewhere. I would do the same, and when I was the one with a boyfriend it would be different—I wouldn't feel abandoned. Emir and I would be on the same page again. And we could discuss our boyfriends. So I honed in on one. At the office. Again.

Patrick was my first Republican.

He was tall and good-looking and articulate and, when he wasn't debating politics or drinking too much at happy hour at the Irish bar across the street, the quiet type. Patrick became my closest confidant at the office and then the friendship turned into something else—a fun secret office romance. He lived with five roommates uptown. Patrick was conservative and reserved, and swore me to secrecy about us—he planned to become a top agent, and he wanted a reputation as a complete professional. I told Patrick I was married, and watched the initial shock fade as I explained what Emir and I were up to. Patrick passed the litmus test, to my surprise; as conservative as he was, he accepted and understood what Emir and I were doing. Emir and I had what we wanted: our boyfriends—though Patrick didn't want the label of boyfriend (which I ignored)—and each other.

I didn't care about Patrick's politics. I cared about him, and no one here was looking to get married. Patrick didn't have to be right for me. We could have a simpler relationship, a friendship with benefits as these things were called, but we didn't label it anything and soon settled into a routine of after-work drinks and casual sex. He wouldn't brand himself my boyfriend and I wouldn't criticize the president. We didn't have "the talk." But I could feel it, and felt certain that he did, too. But could Patrick love a liberal? Could I settle down with a man who had voted for George W. Bush? I took the fact he never minded I was married to Emir for his green card as a sign that these political leanings might not be as important to Patrick as they seemed when he was arguing with Brad in the mailroom—that it was simply rhetoric, not a code of conduct.

Beneath my good-natured, enthused exterior, the mailroom routine was a spiral to a slow and painful soul-death. I rode the freight elevator up with the trash bins. Besides Clippings and sitting at our table, the only other trainee duty was taking the mail carts up the freight elevator four times a day to make the delivery rounds. We were bored. This was a pit stop on the road to a "creative career," I told myself. I watched the lifers, the people (purportedly ex-cons) who worked in the mailroom too, for whom there would be no "getting promoted upstairs," and I tried to feel grateful. While we sat around debating politics and reading the trades, the lifers made photocopies and sorted mail. They pulled apart pieces of chicken with their fingers behind metal shelves during lunch while we went to the Soup Man, aka the "Soup Nazi" from *Seinfeld*, for twelve-dollar lobster bisque.

Emir and I had not heard a thing from the INS. We entered a time when it was easy to forget our purpose, when all we did was live like the young people in our twenties we were, and that was when we stopped paying attention. Since Emir had his Employment Authorization card and could legally work in the United States, we no longer felt the pressure we did when initially deciding to get married. The interview would come up when it was time. We began living as if everything were settled and decided and we were exactly the same as any of the Lower East Side roommates in the apartments below ours and all around, that strange camaraderie of those who live with others because they can't afford to live alone or don't want to be lonely in the sometimes-alienating city.

This was our mistake. We should never have stopped paying attention. When you lose awareness of the potential for bad things to happen, that is when they happen, arriving as if to remind you not to get too comfortable, to jolt you into something else, to lift a curtain and scream. The type of moment commonly known as a wake-up call.

It was early November. In a week I would turn twenty-three. On TV, the President was calling for an end to Iraq's production of weapons of mass destruction. In the mailroom, the rate of Clippings production had slowed significantly as we took to reading the newspapers instead of slicing them up as we were supposed to. Patrick and Brad's political debates intensified, with Patrick arguing that the president was doing the right thing, it was the United States' job to protect the global community. Brad was convinced it was an elaborate revenge plot against Saddam Hussein and we were being lied to.

The news that week informed the world that weapons inspectors had entered Iraq. I agreed with Brad; a war based on lies would soon be underway, with people my age and younger dying over those lies. It made the possibility of a couple getting busted for their marriage even more absurd. The weekend arrived and Patrick was in Connecticut for his father's golf tournament at the country club. I was not invited. It was glaringly obvious by then that he would never want me to meet his parents. On Saturday night, Emir and I decided to go out on an all-nighter. It had been a while since I'd gone out to the clubs with Emir and Drew. It would be a fun respite from being sad about my nonexistent relationship with Patrick.

I don't remember what club it was, but the night grew late and we were drunk. Drew wanted to show us the back room, a secret VIP lounge, and I followed him as he led Emir by the hand toward a door marked exit. This was not a VIP lounge. The room was small and dingy, with walls the color of dried blood. It was the room where people came to do things they couldn't on the outside. A disco ball dangled over the table like an indifferent eye, sprinkling light over the men gathered around the table, lines of white powder in front of them. Cocaine. Sitting on the couches around the coffee table, Drew cut up six lines, two for each of us. Art was not the only thing Drew dealt. He and Emir did their lines, and Emir passed the straw to me. I wondered if we could catch something by sharing the straw but shrugged this off. I took the straw, taking two rapid inhales, and knew that this was not cocaine.

It produced even more euphoric sensations, as if a light switch had flipped in my brain. Right then I knew I could do anything. I was all-powerful, I had been put on the earth for a reason I would never know or understand; all I had to know was that it existed. My heart sped.

I leaned over to shout into Drew's ear.

"What kind of coke is this?" I asked.

"It's not," said Drew. "It's Tina."

"Tina?"

"Crystal!" he shouted over the noise.

"*Meth?*" I yelled back, even though I already knew exactly what he meant.

"I thought you knew," he said. "Sorry."

It was a drug I associated with trailer parks and rotting front teeth. I had no idea its use was spreading in urban gay communities. Soon after, I would notice anti-meth ads posted at bus stops along Eighth Avenue in Chelsea.

After the onslaught of the rush, the thoughtless bliss, I realized that this drug could be very useful. I could run home and churn out a novel by daybreak. There was a secret to having focus—intense, unbreakable, determined focus—and it was this. With this energy I could do anything. I danced and danced until it wore off and was surprised by the shock of daylight when we emerged from the club.

I asked Emir if he had met Tina before, and he said that he hadn't, though Drew saw her recreationally. I had been reading about it online and told him I thought it was too dangerous and addictive. I liked the feeling a little too much—the energy, the motivation, the euphoria—and Emir loved it. Though we said that day we would never do it again, it set something off in us, and woke up an urge I had buried back in L.A., where certain drugs were popular even at cocktail parties because, unlike alcohol, they contained no calories. Tina made me nervous, but Drew could also get cocaine.

Justification went from mine to ours. So we experimented with a little drug. We weren't addicted. We worked, made our livings, Emir had Drew and I sort of had Patrick, though I worried about him. He drank too much and wore the same suit so often it had begun to fray.

Emir and I had our cozy apartment on the Lower East Side to come home to. Our nights out at clubs were nothing more than that; we didn't always buy drugs. Still, I started keeping a little stash. I hid it from Patrick, who would never approve of my bringing coke to work in a tiny baggie stuffed in my lipstick case, but I found that if I added a couple small bumps, taken off the tip of my house key, to my morning routine, it helped me fly through tedious days of mail runs. I learned exactly how much to do, enough to get the energy but not feel jittery, enough that no one would ever suspect anything was up. On weekend nights, I did enough to stay up until dawn so I wouldn't miss anything, but not enough to stay awake all through the following day like Emir did. He wrote two screenplays that month and we were both beginning to frighten me.

A few weeks later, Emir and I had the talk again. If we ended up addicted, our mission to keep him here was never going to work. It had started as recreational, but the more all-nighters, the darker the under-eye circles, the vaguer the explanations of where he'd been made it clear it was deepening; the affair was becoming something else. It was turning into love. Since it bothered me, and he didn't want me to be upset with him, he would not do it again. And this was easy to say because, he reiterated, he could take it or leave it. I suspected he was lying.

On a weekday morning some weeks later, I had my proof. I emerged from my bedroom to find Emir sitting at the kitchen table with his laptop. It was a quarter to seven, my hair was still wet, and I was running late for Clippings.

"Tell me the truth."

Emir peered up at me and I gasped. He looked as if he hadn't slept in days. Dark circles raccooned his big, almond-brown eyes.

"About what?"

"These suit pants. Do they make my thighs look fat?"

"No."

"Were you up all night?"

"Yes."

"Playing Sims?"

"Revising my screenplay."

He went back to clicking away on the keyboard. I stood there frozen. Emir was much too alert that early hour of the morning, when he was usually half-asleep and grumbling under his breath about needing his coffee.

"Emir? Were you really?"

"Yes."

His leg shook.

Are you sure you're all right?"

"I am great! Really great!"

He bounced up and down in his chair as if shaken by an earthquake.

"How is it going?" I asked gently.

"Finishing the final rewrite. This is the best thing I've ever written."

"Emir?"

"Yes, my sweets?"

"You know I love you and I said I'd never leave you as long as your green card was pending, no matter what. But this Tina thing. I can't stand it. I can't stand to see you doing this to yourself. You have everything going for you. Why are you doing this?"

Emir looked up at me and smiled but it was forced, strained.

"Thank you for worrying," he said. "You know you are loved by a person who worries so much about you."

"I just want to make sure you're okay."

"I am. How is Patrick?"

I rolled my eyes. "Still Republican, possibly alcoholic, and I think I might be in love with him."

"Right."

"I don't like Drew."

"Excuse me?"

I had crossed a line. Friends don't tell friends they don't like their boyfriends until the relationship ends—otherwise you're the bad guy. But I kept going.

"I don't trust him. He's not good for you. Look at what's happening. It's disgusting. I think you should break up with him."

"Of all people."

"What?"

"Of all people, how could *you* judge me? What's the difference between coke and Tina anyway? You're the real poster girl for healthful living."

I'd done it, struck a nerve. The moment I said it I knew I'd intended this. I wanted a reaction. He turned back to the screen and resumed typing away, pounding the keys as if he intended to break them. A lump rose in my throat and I gulped it back down as if swallowing a knife.

"If you don't stop," I said, "I'll have no choice but to consider divorce."

"I haven't done anything!" he lied. "I just have a lot of ideas right now."

"How can we pretend to be married when we aren't even honest enough to be friends?" I yelled, slamming the apartment door behind me, my face flushed hot as I took the six flights of stairs so quickly and carelessly in high heels I almost fell.

On the F train I pulled out a book to read but the words blurred through the tears that fell on the page. I'd known it and yet I looked the other way. And who was I but a hypocrite for telling him not to take drugs when we did them together? Idealism and empathy dissolved that morning. I'd had it. Something needed to change and if it wasn't going to be him, it would be me.

I knew that no matter what, I couldn't, wouldn't ever file for divorce. My ultimatum was an empty threat. I loved him too much. He could destroy everything right in front of me and still I wouldn't let him go. But I had to do something.

When I came home from Patrick's on Sunday evening, Emir was crying in the kitchen. I pulled up a chair beside him.

"What happened now?"

"Drew has been cheating on me."

It was Adrian and The Kid all over again, though Adrian, while unfaithful, didn't send chills down my spine with his mere presence. I hated seeing Emir hurt again but secretly I felt hopeful that this spelled the end of the destructive relationship.

"One time or ongoing?"

Emir looked at me and I knew.

"It seems like the end of the world right now, but you're going to be fine."

It would be many things but fine wasn't one of them.

It was getting cold again and Emir had the flu. I was relieved. The flu would keep him in. It would keep him from his lover, their drama, and their mistress Tina, at least for a few days. I brought him tea, juice, and cold medicine while he was laid up. I blamed Drew. In the two weeks Emir was sick, Drew made himself scarce.

Some things we can choose not to see until, gradually, the thing absolutely insists that we face it.

Drew called Emir a few weeks later. Emir had hoped it was an apology. I thought he missed Drew less than he missed being in a relationship, any relationship, a warm body to sleep next to, arms in which to be held. "Love-fools." Emir had been the one to call us that. Anything for the men in our lives—anything, especially, to win back one we'd lost.

That wasn't why Drew was calling. Drew was calling to say he had tested positive for HIV. He was contacting all his old lovers. Emir and Drew had unprotected sex because they were monogamous, or at least Emir had thought so. Only then did I find out the details of Drew's cheating. Drew had been going to underground parties and having sex with different men; reckless, unprotected sex, because on meth you didn't care. Nothing was real and actions were without consequences.

The news hit me like a fist to the stomach, the wind knocked

out of me—this was Emir's life at stake—but the legal circumstances immediately followed as my mind went the immigration
route. If Emir was HIV-positive, he could not get a green card.
It was against the law. Being HIV-positive still disqualified a
foreigner even from entering the United States at all.

Life as an HIV-positive man in Emiristan would be worse
than anything I ever imagined as a possible outcome for our
marriage and immigration situation. It was easy to blame
myself. If only we hadn't moved to New York. If only I hadn't
been so foolish in our early days. We would not have come to
New York and Emir would never have met Drew. What could I
have said or done to prevent this? I blamed myself. I caused this.
I'd later see the self-blame as another form of narcissism. Who
was I to think I had any control over Emir's life or choices, or
that anything happened directly because of a decision I made?
I screwed up a lot early in our marriage but only Emir could
decide what Emir did.

"I'm scared," said Emir. I was too and hoped, for once, that
we were both wrong.

12.

Caged Birds

"AIDS raised the emotionally charged question of
who counted as family in the most profound ways."
—Chauncey

Awaiting the results, afterward we sat on a bench in the small
park by the Christopher Street subway station, surrounded by
statues of people sitting on benches. I sat with my arm around
Emir, also like a statue.

Looking back it made sense: the chronic bouts of flu, the
dark circles. I had thought he was still doing meth. HIV had
never occurred to me. It wasn't something I ever considered
a possibility, so naïve was I then. Posters connecting meth use
to HIV exposure were only plastered all over the bus stops in
Chelsea. I thought of that Tower tarot card, the one I'd drawn
September 10th. Was a warning a warning a warning even
when the circumstances changed, even when time passed?

I wasn't sure where we would go from here—what it would

mean for the green card we still awaited. Our INS interview wasn't scheduled yet. The medical exam—we had to look at the expiration date on the medical exam. There could still be hope if we were called for our interview before that date. This was the only way around deportation. The exam results would be valid for three more months; if we were called before then, Emir could slide between the bureaucratic cracks. He called our lawyer. Was there anything we could do to speed the process? Our lawyer wanted to know why and Emir told him. The lawyer was empathetic and promised to maintain confidentiality and try his best.

How had it come to this? Emir was the organized, rational one in our twosome—I was the one who brought the chaos. I was the mess. How did it all get so turned around?

When Emir was going off the rails, he kept it concealed to a degree that I really believed he was through with the drugs, though denial or simply ignorance on my part was also likely. What I had gone through in high school was so similar, using by night and functioning every day. Only the young body could tolerate this kind of life, and even then, I'm surprised I simply came out of it; I was a dabbler, a dilettante, even with drugs. Coated in that adolescent shroud of invincibility as my friends and I arrived at a point when we were sprinkling cocaine into our before-school cigarettes, I somehow came out unharmed.

The results came in. It was not HIV, but we were not off the hook that easily. There was a diagnosis, something likely also passed to Emir by Drew. I learned that there was a list of infectious diseases that barred foreigners from entering or immigrating to the U.S. and Emir now had two of them. Our lawyer told us that if Emir was required to retake the medical exam, these, too, would stand in the way of his green card. The HIV scare was a reality check for us both—the reality of mortality and the ultimate damage a bad relationship could cause.

If it was ever going to end badly, I imagined it would be with our flags flying high, being led away in handcuffs, broadcast on the news, written about in the newspapers: visa chief's daughter arrested for fraudulent immigration marriage. I never imagined it could be something worse.

I had to go to the office the next morning in the cold, sleet, and rain. I was sent to cover the phone at the CEO's sixteenth-floor desk. Patrick was doing the early 16A mail run. He brought me a mug of coffee from the kitchen. I thanked him and told him it was exactly what I needed. I hadn't slept much the night before.

"Did you go out?" he asked.

"Emir found out he has two infections that could keep him from getting his green card," I said.

I was feeling open and vulnerable and realized I needed to talk to someone about it. I would have told my mother, would have wanted to lean on her, but I feared her judgment.

"Did you ever sleep with him?" Patrick asked, his hazel eyes bulging with worry.

I understood why he would want to know, but I also felt offended—sex with my best friend? He may as well have insinuated I'd been sleeping with my brother. And all of that aside, why would he think I'd go sleeping around when all I wanted was to be committed to *him*?

Patrick and I grew apart after that. He ended things with me at a bar on the Lower East Side a week later. "This isn't going anywhere," he said. We both knew. He left alone, drunk, and I followed him from a distance to Ray's Pizza on Houston, where he sat down and ate a slice. I realized it was the first time I ever saw him eat anything. It was as if we had never been together in the first place.

Crisis reveals what a relationship really is, either driving you closer or breaking you apart. Where Patrick and I were headed was clear. What would happen with Emir was far murkier and much more important.

The small apartment Emir and I shared had gone from a warm, colorful place of animated banter, shared takeout, and fun to sepia-toned, somber, a place that felt as if someone—or something, some bit of youth, optimism, and naïveté—had recently died. When I returned from the mailroom, Emir and I didn't eat Chinese food or exchange funny stories. An obsession with what we could control—the organization and order of our apartment, our home—led us to a winter cleaning binge. We donated old clothes, dusted shelves and the insides of drawers. We coped with wine, with silence, with small talk, until one night, when we were done cleaning, Emir pulled his photo collection from the top shelf of his closet.

We collapsed on the bed and he spread them around, picking out a family portrait of his mother and father with his two younger sisters and him. In the picture, Emir wears the same yellow turtleneck as in another shot he showed me in his dorm room three years before. How had it only been three years?

Emir stared at the photograph. "They would never have wanted this for me," he said. "They would be so disappointed."

I didn't know what to say, so I said I was sorry.

We were silent for a moment.

"I'm so ashamed," he said. "And what if I have to do the exam again? What if the INS finds out?"

"It's going to work out."

"What if it doesn't?"

I longed to comfort him but when I thought of what I would usually do to uplift a brokenhearted friend—hugs, cups of tea, a listening ear, cocktails, or comfort food—they all seemed insufficient.

Emir was an uninsured freelancer at the time of his diagnosis, working his latest job as a production assistant on a movie about, of all subjects, Alfred Kinsey. Emir knew it had to be his last freelance job. Health insurance was no longer optional. I wasn't sure why we had never put him on mine.

Emir rationalized ending the work he loved by telling himself that the fixed schedule and reliable income the office gave him would allow him to carve out more time for screenwriting. He sent his scripts out and they placed as finalists in major competitions, but he hadn't won, not yet.

Emir's friend El Toro, who moved to Montreal after September 11th, had a former boss who had a friend who owned a gay porn-and-photography studio in Chelsea, MuscleNet. They specialized in art photos of bodybuilders. The porn was more of a side project and not hardcore, mainly images of bodybuilders masturbating, nothing too scandalous. Emir was hired as the office manager. He dealt with accounting and invoices and budgets. He kept things running smoothly. He didn't have contact with the actual porn aspect of the company's dealings, but the editing suite was in an adjacent room and he could hear all the moans and groans as he filled phone orders and filed invoices. I visited him at his new job—he had a beautiful office by a floor-to-ceiling window that faced the Empire State Building. From the perspective of someone who worked in a basement, it was nothing short of glorious.

During the weeks that followed, Emir went to doctors' appointments and got medication. After the health scare, I realized that all along, I had been imagining that we had magical powers of some sort—no one at the INS would doubt the authenticity of our marriage, that we would eventually find the loves of our lives, that someday Emir could come out to his family and I could tell my mother what we'd done, and they would fully accept us as we were.

This was the romantic comedy version of our story, that no matter how twisted the plot became, how messy the ride, the tension was pleasurable because in the end, of course, everything was going to work out for the young protagonists, because they were only hitting the usual plot points, having a few confrontations and minor disasters in order to learn some lessons on their way to growing up, both as individuals and within their whole

*Odd Couple, I Love Lucy, Will & Grace*-on-steroids slapstick as they barreled along toward their inevitable happy ending.


My period was two weeks late. At first I wasn't worried. Stress changed my cycle and I attributed the late cycle to the stress surrounding Emir's diagnosis. The stress of wondering if my best friend, my support system—my husband—would be taken from me if the medical exam he did back in L.A. expired before we were called for our interview, and that was assuming we were approved right away. Emir's diagnosis made me more careful about things, so we walked to Rite Aid in the rain anyway, huddled together beneath one umbrella, to procure a pregnancy test for me "just to make sure." Cabs splashed us from puddles on the edges of First Avenue. Inside the drugstore, lite FM played as I perused the shelves: Clearview, First Response, Aim MidStream, Rite Aid brand.

"Do you think there's much difference between one or another?"

"They seem the same to me," said Emir.

I picked up the least expensive, the generic. Back in the apartment, I peed on the stick, washed my hands, placed the stick on the edge of the sink and left the room, closing the bathroom door behind me. I could not walk back in after the two minutes had passed. I didn't think there would be two pink lines, but if there were, I didn't want the shock of first seeing them. I wanted Emir to look.

"Will you look?" I mumbled.

"Are you sure?"

"You're right. I should do this. Okay."

I took a deep breath and went back in.

When I came back out, my lips must have gone white because Emir asked what I was going to do.

What *was* I going to do? I tried to imagine living in a house in Connecticut with Patrick and a baby. I couldn't. The positive pregnancy test reminded me of what Emir and I used to say about having a child—if neither of us ever met anybody we fell in love with and wanted to start a family with—via artificial insemination. I thought of how that would never happen now. Or if I had this baby, how it still could. Emir and I could raise her. Mohammad would be excited to learn of my pregnancy and Emir could say it was his.

I was stunned silent.

"Is it Patrick's?" Emir asked.

"He's the only person I've recently had sex with . . ."

"Unprotected?"

"No, we used condoms. They're not foolproof, obviously. Do you think I need to tell him?"

"I don't know, sweetie. Anything about your body is such a personal choice . . . do you think you need to tell him?"

"I don't want to. He's all pro-life and stuff."

"Do you want to have that baby?"

"It's not a baby yet and I don't know."

Having just found out, I felt it was too much to take in—being pregnant at twenty-three, having to decide whether to end the pregnancy or try to have the baby. If Emir and I raised her together and Patrick visited and Mohammad helped with child support . . . but what would I tell my mother? I wasn't even sure I wanted kids; could I really go and have one in an unplanned pregnancy with a guy who wasn't even my boyfriend?

The HIV scare and other diagnosis, the pregnancy—were our impulses to self-sabotage stronger than those to preserve? One was a disease that took life, the other a condition that perpetuated it, and yet these unrelated physical conditions seemed to mirror each other as Emir and I did; unrelated, happening at the same time . . .

Patrick was against abortion. Having a baby at twenty-three while married to Emir was a terrible idea. All our talk about artificial insemination, maybe raising a child together one day, was only that: talk. We each wanted more traditional lives with men we loved. We had been joking and pretending we weren't, not serious while pretending we were being playful. We could have done it, it could have worked, but when it came down to it, it wasn't what either of us wanted, at least not then.

"You're lucky," Emir said, "that it's your decision what to do, whether you have an abortion or not, whether you tell him or not. Where I'm from you don't have a choice."

Emir came with me to the clinic in a Brooklyn office building. Here was another bureaucratic process—take a number, get in line, have a quick procedure, go home. Women in sweat suits lined up on wooden benches against the wall.

"Your boyfriend can come in with you if you want," a nurse said.

"He can?" I asked.

"We allow one companion in the room."

Emir and I looked at each other and both shook our heads.

Emir waited in the waiting room and helped me into bed when we got home. He climbed in after me and held me there.

Sign on the New York City subway: *Abortion Changes You.* For a free country, there were an awful lot of people who wanted to limit our choices. I lay in bed afterward, unsure if I was changed.

# Part III:
# Show Business

13.

The Real Big Day

"In the modern jambalaya of online dating, arranged weddings, bicoastal relationships, open marriages and serial divorce, a bona fide union can be harder than ever to discern."

—Nina Bernstein, *The New York Times*

Day by day, the August air grew heavier. That summer of 2003 brought one of the worst electrical blackouts in the country's history, leaving the city in darkness. Our street was filled with the smell of the garbage piled in black trash bags on the sidewalk again. I was promoted at work, out of the mailroom to a position in something I was already an expert at—floating. The floater position entailed being an internal temp. (William Morris didn't deal with outside temp agencies. Too much confidential information was at stake, mostly about celebrities' movie and TV deals.) There was always a job but no desk. I worked for different agents whenever their regular assistants were sick or on vacation. I was a clerical understudy. Patrick had a permanent job in the television department, representing anchors for Fox

News. Gay marriage was becoming a topic of national discussion. Many of the people I'd started with in the mailroom had left the company. The day of the Northeastern blackout, work was cancelled; I joined a swarm of people walking downtown on Second Avenue, overhearing conversations about how much like 9/11 this was. Once we learned it wasn't terrorism, Emir and I split a bag of mushrooms and played backgammon in Tompkins Square Park all afternoon. At night, the city felt wild. Drum circles formed on street corners, along with a feeling of community that was absent from the electrified world.

Monday evenings were reserved for therapy and Therapy. We tried to make the best of things, to cope through our shared sense of humor.

The first was with a couples' therapist referred by a man in a support group Emir attended. We met with him in his West Village office to talk through how we were doing. The sessions began with ordinary complaints: how Emir annoyed me, talking to me while I was trying to write and being too nitpicky about the cleanliness of our apartment. Emir was frustrated by my habit of never showing up on time—which the therapist attributed to my lack of relationship with my father, citing something Jungian about "Father Time"—or forgetting to pick up the laundry when it was my week. After the ice-breaking venting, we got down to the real business of how we were both coping with the trauma of Emir's diagnoses. As a couple of sorts (the therapist knew we were married—patient confidentiality also meant we could tell him why) it deeply affected me, too, more than I was consciously aware of, the therapist said.

I talked about the marriage, how I'd gone into it thinking it would be the most uncomplicated of arrangements, that Emir and I would live together and have fun, carefree, creative lives of work, boyfriends, and family, and then he would get his green card, and I would get a friend for life. I could not have imagined, at the outset, that my gift would lead to the wrong relationship that potentially robbed him of years of his life.

"It seems there is a lot of self-blame on both your parts," our therapist said. "We have to get you out of the cycle—blame isn't healthy whether on yourself or your partner."

Easy for him to say. If only I had never fallen for the book thief, if only we had never moved to New York, if only I hadn't been the one who really wanted to go out the night Emir ended up meeting Drew. All of this could have been so easily avoided.

We emerged onto the West Village street, where a strong, chilly wind bowed the bare arms of small trees, and walked to the subway in silence. Therapy with a capital T was where we went to relax after the first kind. We got on the subway and shuttled to Hell's Kitchen to go to the gay bar, because we wanted to feel as though humor still played a role in all of this. Therapy was filled with beautiful men in sleek high-fashion outfits. The drinks had names like Psychotic Episode, Pavlov's Dog, and Freudian Sip. Most of them were sweet, our preference for cocktails and men. I got drunk on Denial, a sugary mix of Absolut and fruit juices; and denial, the refusal to recognize and acknowledge.

Denial didn't last. Emir opened the mailbox in the vestibule when we got home and there was a letter addressed to him from the U.S. Government. Department of Immigration and Naturalization. We had finally been called for our interview.

We still needed rings. We took the F train uptown to find the Diamond District on 47th Street. We still marveled at the little pockets of New York—"this street is all diamonds! And that other one was all flowers!"—and wandered from store to store for a while, scoping the merchandise before we picked out our rings. I was fine with getting the most inexpensive ones we could find, but Emir had other ideas. "Rings matter," he said. He cited the INS interview as justification, that cheap rings could indicate fake marriage, but I knew his taste for the finer things was really behind it; I shared it, too.

In the windows were rows and rows of diamond rings, engagement rings. Many resembled the ring from Julian, the marquise diamond he picked out because it was more unique than a simple round one. Like you, he said. I wondered where we would have been if it hadn't ended. I didn't know if I had regrets. I had mixed feelings about the concept. On one hand, regret means you've lived long enough to recognize past mistakes; on the other, what's the use?

I chose a simple band of white gold.

It was exactly how a wedding ring should look. I wondered what my mother had done with hers, what it had looked like, and if it was still in a box somewhere. Emir's choice was a thick band, braided in eighteen-karat gold and platinum. That's what happens when you marry a gay man, or when you marry Emir; he ends up with the prettier ring.

The rings cost over a thousand dollars.

"It's too much!" I protested, but Emir pulled out Mohammad's credit card.

"He wants us to have nice rings."

"He also wants us to have his grandson! That doesn't mean you do it!"

But it was too late, and I couldn't do anything about Emir's ongoing struggle about his financial relationship with his father. He didn't want the money, until he did. I understood because I was the same. He signed the slip and we put the bands on each other's ring fingers. I liked my pretty new ring. We agreed we'd only put them on when we had to, but it felt cool and expensive on my finger. I never wore jewelry. Instead I ascribed outrageous value to those odd things that made it through all the years of travels, the matchbooks and postcards and books bought from street vendors, written in languages I didn't speak or understand.

On our way back to the subway, Emir and I pushed through crowds of jewelry shoppers and the Hasidic men who owned and worked in the shops. Sitting side by side on the orange plastic seats, we grabbed at each other's hands and mooned over the rings.

"We should say that the gold and platinum braided together represents the interweaving of our souls," I deadpanned.

"I never imagined wearing one of these," Emir said. "I like it."

"What about me, do you still like me?"

"I love you, wifey."

"Do you promise?"

"Yes, I promise."

"More than ever?"

Emir sighed.

"Yes, more than ever, but you are beginning to annoy me."

When the train rolled into 23rd Street, we decided not to return to the apartment, to keep going. As a kid I begged my mother to let us ride all the way sometimes, past our stop until the D.C. subway ran aboveground, over the Arlington Cemetery, toward unseen places called New Carrollton or Vienna. It was the idea more than the actual spaces, which predictably turned out to be commuter parking lots and railway yards, getting to an endpoint, something that seemed impossible in actuality, when we were constantly thinking ahead to the next place, the next stop, the next trip, the next school, the next life.

The morning of the INS interview, my alarm went off at five-thirty. Stupefied with sleep, it took me a moment to remember why it was buzzing when it was still dark outside. I hit the snooze button.

"Sweetie!" Emir called. He walked in with two mugs of coffee and set them down on the bedside table. "It's the big day!"

The second big day in our first year of marriage.

"Two more minutes," I begged.

He pulled me out of bed by my ankles, as I'd told him to if I had to wake up extra-early and was acting stubborn. My toes touched the floor and I heaved up to standing.

"There you go," he said.

The apartment was freezing. Emir handed me the mug and we shuffled out into the kitchen.

Typically I arose two hours later to my daily routine: shower, put on a suit that still made me feel like a kid dressing as an office lady for Halloween, and was frustrated that yet again I hadn't left enough time to take the subway as I shelled out another fifteen dollars I couldn't afford for a taxi to Midtown and my floater job. I thought, in those days, that if I wasn't married to Emir my life would be so empty. And not only because the marriage still kept my spirit of rebellion alive even after I had technically become a responsible adultlike person, rising for work and home for dinner, collecting a paycheck and talking to my mother every Sunday on the phone; but also because Emir could make me smile, cheer me up when I was sad, and make me feel loved even after I had been dumped. He made me feel understood, and he also made me feel I understood him, I could truly connect with another person—a person I was excited to see even though I saw him every day. We fought and forgave each other. We cried and comforted each other. How was the INS going to build a case against that?

We sat at the kitchen table as the sun peeked over the jagged-teeth horizon of buildings to the west, amazed that the day we had anticipated for so long and prepared for so carefully had arrived. This was the day that determined our outcome; either he would get the green card, and this portion of our journey would have its happy ending, or they would call up our case for further investigation, and we'd have to pull out all the stops, all the evidence, all the people who had seen us through along the way.

Emir looked good in his suit and tie, handsome. Sexual attraction would be easy to fake. For the first time I noted that he looked older now than when I met him. I wondered if I did, too. He had the rings and showed them to me as he'd since had them engraved, without my knowledge, as a surprise for today.

Mine read: *L&Em-Vegas-Frvr.*

His: *99toEternity-imYrs.*

"Cute," I said. "Are you nervous?"

The question reminded me of our wedding day.

"As nervous as you, I imagine," he said.

The penalties for alien smuggling can be found in Section 274 of the Immigration and Nationality Act. According to the law, I had "transported an alien within the United States" (moving from L.A. to New York), "harbored an alien" (in a hipster village called the Lower East Side), and "encouraged or induced an alien to reside in the United States" (*I won't let you go back to a country where you could be killed*). These actions were grounds for fines of up to twenty-five thousand dollars and/or imprisonment of up to ten years.

According to the fine print I was guilty of "reckless disregard," disregarding a risk I "should have known" about helping an "alien" remain in America. Was I concealing, harboring, or shielding Emir from detection by marrying him, even though it was an act of love? It was open for interpretation, and this, too, frightened me. I had definitely encouraged and induced.

The risk wore on me heavily that morning, in a taxi

downtown, on our way to the INS office. But I also felt resigned. This would either work or it wouldn't. No one but me was responsible for the events of the day. The marriage had been my suggestion, my idea for a solution for Emir and for me. I would stand in front of judges and say that as many times as necessary. They could balk at my logic and sentence me to prison. I believed in what I was doing. I still believe it was the right decision, and I have no regrets about having married Emir.

I search and search and find that I have many feelings and that remorse is not one of them. I wish I could launch into a complicated, nuanced explanation of denial and youthful ignorance, but that is not who I am, and perhaps that is what allowed me to marry Emir in the first place. The younger girl must have been out of touch with what was going on, right? That this was about safety without the intimacy of sex?

Maybe I will never be a real adult, but are there any real adults? Or maybe the "real adult" is only a construct of childhood, a fantasy, nonexistent. We'd been through a lot and I wanted us to get through our own personal judgment day as a couple, too. Live through it, no matter what.

We passed through metal detectors. The fluorescent-lit waiting room smelled of half-eaten breakfast sandwiches, coffee, and the nerves of a thousand immigrants. It reminded me of the time Emir and I went to sign up for Central Casting in L.A., and of the summer I worked with my mom in Mexico City, where I first learned about immigration and how agents detect fraud. Similar questions ran through my head as at the Las Vegas marriage license office: which of these couples were in green card marriages? The Hispanic man with the blonde lady? The portly guy in the Yankees hat, who sat with a child? Who would be approved, and who would be escorted away to a holding room for further questioning, and who would be sent home and required to report back at a later date? The room was full of people and I cannot remember any of their faces. My stomach felt as if it were going to escape by squeezing up through my throat and out my mouth.

*Even if they haul me away in shackles today I will go screaming and yelling in defense of my decision to marry Emir and the relationship we have,* I wrote in my diary in the waiting room.

Promising to polish each other's blue suede shoes in front of an Elvis impersonator was nothing compared to this. Here was cold, stark, bureaucratic reality. It resembled my mother's offices, fluorescent-lit and harsh, ugly industrial furniture. Not that it should have been a spa with pitchers of lemon-and-cucumber water, but did it have to feel like a human factory? I memorized Allen Ginsberg's poem "America" in high school in Mexico City because everyone had to memorize a poem and I wanted to choose one that spoke to me, that felt as if it were addressing me personally. *Businessmen are serious. Movie producers are serious. Everybody's serious but me.*

You can't be serious—you're invoking your teen angst *now*, at a time like this? I chided myself.

What if I couldn't separate from my younger self, because *that younger self was still me?* Because people don't change, they become more complicated and self-assured versions of the same selves, as they grow independent and comfortable in charge of their own little worlds within the world.

My mother caught alien smugglers all the time. She said she could sniff them out, so honed was her skill set. My mother the spy. I recalled my favorite Jung quote again, that things of which we are not conscious manifest in our lives as fate. So what did it mean that I became close with Emir, a man who would need to find a means of staying in the United States, and that I offered my own hand in marriage while it was my mother's career to prevent that very thing?

It was a puzzle that did not lend itself to easy solution. Possibly it was coincidence, and these two things were not connected. But my feeling was they were. It was too perfect, a reality stranger than fiction.

I felt as if the rebellion of my teenage years had not waned, but exploded.

Was I still playing out my rebellion against my mother? Did I harbor some unconscious resentment of her moving me around throughout my childhood? I was constantly focused on acclimating to entirely different ways of life, new cultures, foreign languages. It's good to be adaptable, she said, and it was. I'd adapted so well, even to my role as Emir's wife.

I did not want them to judge us but that's what we were here for. I'd known this coming in but once the actual moment arrived I felt more nervous than I ever had about anything before. It was impossible to know then if it would be an in-and-out take-a-number type of event, or end in a string of accusations.

My thoughts grew increasingly abstract as I sat in a hard

plastic chair, wedged between Emir and a stranger, in that
waiting room crammed full of bleary-eyed hopeful citizens at
seven in the morning that was loud in a way only silence can
be. *Are we going to be okay? We were always perfect on paper.* Why
weren't they calling our names? What was taking so long? The
medical exam could expire while we were still sitting here.

"Should've brought a sleeping bag," I muttered.

"*Shhh . . .*" Emir hushed me.

Emir seemed intimidated. I know I was.

We all were.

All of us.

Anonymity united by a common purpose.

"Remember, if it comes up at all . . . you're not gay, you're
just foreign," I whispered.

Emir nodded and peered at a newspaper. He wasn't reading.

"Your lips are white," he whispered.

I pulled out a compact mirror. They were indeed. I rubbed on
some burgundy-colored balm and sat quietly like a good girl in
my bureaucratic chair. Legs crossed, proper attire, chin in palm,
elbow propped on raised knee. I waited there like a statue or an
eighteenth-century lady, sitting for a portrait. A poster on the
wall reminded us to "*Celebrate Citizenship, Celebrate America.*"

I was going through with this the same way I had followed
through with every stage that came before: proposal, wedding,
moving in, joint accounts, checking the Married box on those
tax forms, and staying the course through the ups and downs,
just like a real marriage. If it all imploded this day, would my
mother come to my aid? Could she? She had close ties in the
INS. Maybe Mom would swoop in, full-on spy-superhero

mode in a cape and Zorro mask, to save the day? Maybe she had known and been on our side all along?

Anyone else here marrying a gay friend they could not stand to see sent back to an intolerant homeland?

*Anyone?*

It all came back to the same question—how do you prove love? Emir and I could kiss and touch each other in front of the officer, would that be proof? Or they could come over and see our clothes mixed together in the closets. What evidence would prove we were regular people living regular lives? Would we have to know the color of each other's toothbrushes? Mine was purple. Emir's was white with a green stripe. They sat beside each other in the toothbrush holder above the sink. So what if we could say that? What did it really mean?

Our names were called and we were escorted back through a mazelike configuration of offices and cubicles, and into an inner office where we sat down again, this time in padded blue armchairs. We were told the officer would be right with us. We clutched our photo albums and document portfolios. I was sweating. Beads of sweat formed around Emir's hairline, on his forehead.

The door opened and clicked shut and there he was: the man who would determine our future.

He was a white man, mid-fifties I'd guess, average weight, height, build. He had a face, I don't remember it. Hair, graying. Eyes, blue.

The man sat behind his desk piled high with files and folders, now holding our lives in his hands, our lives in the form of our history as retold by documentation. Let's call him Gary Kubiak.

Gary Kubiak, INS officer. Your average middle-aged white

male, mustache, ruddy complexion, reddish-brown hair, a wife and two kids at home on Staten Island or in Babylon. Could have been a cop or a fireman. Good guy. Hosts a wicked barbecue. Does not know any gay people, at least not any who are out. American flag waving from his front porch.

Gary Kubiak asked us how we were doing and we said we were doing fine. We asked him the same and he repeated the same back at us.

*He knows,* was all I could think. *He knows.*

Knows what? Something. That Emir is gay. That something about us was different, and different was not good. And in his business, something different means something wrong. I was a little too close to home in this office. Gary Kubiak opened a file on his desk, took our packet of forms, photographs, and miscellanea, and started looking through it. I saw our framed picture of us riding the Stratosphere after our wedding and the others of kissing in front of Elvis, of us at the Stinking Rose restaurant where we ate garlic ice cream for Emir's twenty-third birthday shortly before we moved to New York.

"So how did you two meet?"

"College," Emir and I echoed.

"Emerson College. In Boston," I added.

"College sweethearts," Gary Kubiak repeated.

"Yes, sir," said Emir.

"That's nice. Married my high school sweetheart, myself."

Emir and I talked about how lucky we were to have found each other so young. He wasn't bullshitting. After growing up changing friends every few years, I, too, was lucky to have been able to keep him with me, to not have to say good-bye.

Gary Kubiak continued.

"When is your wedding anniversary?"

"November seventeenth, two thousand and one," we said in unison.

"So soon after September eleventh," he added.

*Would you be saying that if he weren't from a Muslim country?* I wondered.

"Yes, we were engaged before and had planned on that date," Emir said.

But in that moment he sounded unsure of himself, as if he were trying to find exactly the right words and say precisely the correct thing.

"All right, and why did you move to New York?"

"Work opportunities," I said.

"What kind?"

"I . . . my uncle runs a theater company. We had the chance to work in marketing and publicity for them."

"And you don't do that anymore."

"They don't have money. I work at William Morris and my husband—"

"I know where you work. My next question is why is there a note in your file regarding a call to our tip line about you two having married solely for the gentleman's green card?"

*Oliver?* I wondered, my heart racing. Who knew? It could have been any number of people who knew Emir and I were married but he was gay. I tried to hide my panic. My heart flopped wildly in my chest cavity. Emir looked green.

"Probably an ex-boyfriend with a personal grudge," I said.

Who? Oliver? Julian? JULIAN? I hated that I thought that

it could have been Julian. I tried to dismiss it. *Impossible. He wouldn't. Would he? Would Julian do that?*

How well can you ever really know another person?

"Mister al-Habibi?"

"Look at all our things," he said. "Look at the pictures. The lease for our apartment. Mail, bank account . . . this is my best friend from college, sir! Everything you need as proof is there, sir. I love my wife."

"And I love my husband," I said. "Come over and do a home visit, you'll see."

Gary Kubiak fell silent. He stared. He leaned forward. His belly folded over his belt. Our documents were spread all over his desk and he proceeded to review them one by one. He got us to feel comfortable by asking simple, straightforward questions and *then* threw the curveball. My mother recovered stolen property that way, solved overseas kidnapping cases, and saw straight through immigration fraud. If I told Gary Kubiak who she was and to please call her to clear up any confusion, would she back me up? I wasn't sure. Nothing felt certain at all, not that it had in the first place.

"If you did marry for a green card, and I personally am not accusing you of that, you sure covered yourselves. Your records are airtight."

"We did what was required, sir," Emir said.

"But we do have the matter of the anonymous complaint."

"It's a lie," I said.

"Say the police get a phone call saying that an individual is forming a terrorism plot. It could be baloney but they have to investigate that individual. It's that kind of scenario."

I didn't have to look in a mirror to know what color my lips were.

"Are you aware that taking shortcuts to get a green card is illegal and marrying under false pretenses is grounds for arrest?" said Gary Kubiak.

"Can't you see you are making her cry?" my husband said.

He put his arms around me and I folded into him, sobbing.

"Does she have something to cry about?" Gary Kubiak asked.

"She's sensitive," Emir said. "She cries all the time."

I looked up and nodded.

"It's true! I'm oversensitive."

"She always has been," Emir said.

"Do you know the definition of marriage fraud?" Gary Kubiak asked. "It is exploitation, first and foremost. Marriage fraud is faking that you're in love with somebody to get or keep them in the country. Does this in any way describe you?"

If I was committing exploitation, why was it I who felt exploited?

"No," we said.

I wiped my face with my sleeve.

"How regularly do you engage in sexual relations?"

I had been dreading that question. All my bravado melted away, bravery was gone. I had been reduced to this blubbering mess in an immigration office in downtown Manhattan.

"We love sex," Emir said.

*Well-phrased, Emir.* We did love sex, we just didn't have it with each other. All a matter of semantics. Gary Kubiak looked at me. I cleared my throat.

"Yes, we are very sexually active."

Gary Kubiak seemed to consider this.

"Look, I'm on your side here," he said. "I can see your relationship—years of doing this like I have, you develop a sixth sense for it, and you're not about a green card. If it were up to me I would approve your case today. You add up on paper and I can see you guys are good. I'm sure you won't mind if I ask you a question or two in private."

He turned to Emir. "Will you come with me for a moment?"

I looked at Emir and he looked at me, both of us quietly panicked and trying to hide it. Why was he separating us? What was going to happen? It was something out of the movie *Green Card*, and now it was something out of my life.

I was alone in the room.

Gary Kubiak returned. He sat down at his desk across from me. He looked me in the eye.

"Tell me," he said. "Is your husband circumcised?"

*Oh, my God.* Was this legal? Did I have to answer? Was he going to ask Emir to drop his pants? I panicked. *Think, think, think.* In our handful of years of friendship and marriage, Emir and I had never seen each other naked. Another thing we had in common was our modesty. We changed in our rooms. We dressed at least in shorts and T-shirts if we were out in the kitchen area. Neither of us had ever even walked in on the other using the bathroom or in the shower.

I had no idea if Emir was circumcised. I'd never seen his penis.

"Is that a legitimate question?" I said.

"Tell me," he said, "and we can move this right along."

Tears welled in my eyes.

"Why do I have to talk about my husband's private parts with you? How is this not sexual harassment? Can you get a supervisor?"

"I am the supervisor," he said. "So. Circumcised or not?"

*What do I do? Coin toss?*

"Why don't you come visit us at home? Look through our things. See our bedroom, where we sleep, and our office, where we work," I squeaked.

"Are you not answering my question because you do not in fact know if your own husband is circumcised or not?"

*Cut or uncut, as Emir says it's called in the gay world.*

*Had he ever told me?*

"Please don't take him away from me," I said quietly.

"I'm beginning to wonder if you might be lying."

He got up and left the room. I sat there sweating. That's it, I thought. Emir is getting deported, I'm about to be arrested, my mother is going to find out, my life as I know it is over. I tried to prepare myself for the worst but how does one prepare for being shackled and led away to prison? I looked around for an escape route, any escape route. There was none. Kubiak was probably putting Emir in handcuffs at that very moment. All over a Russian Roulette–style question about a penis.

This whole thing . . . what a terrible idea. I should have known it would come to this. Since we didn't have sex, it somehow didn't count as a marriage. It was fake. It didn't feel fake . . . I suddenly understood how people being told by the government that their most important relationship was illegitimate and unrecognizable must feel. This is why I didn't tell my mother; not only because she would be angry and feel betrayed, but also because she would tell me what I couldn't stand to hear: that there was no way Emir and I could make anybody see our marriage as real, least of all a trained INS officer. As usual, I had to go and make mistakes for myself. I wouldn't have taken her advice.

Gary Kubiak came back in. Emir was with him. Not hand-cuffed. Gary Kubiak sat back down and pushed our photo albums across the desk, keeping the rest.

"How long does the investigation typically take?" Emir asked.

"You're investigating us?" I asked.

Kubiak leaned back in his chair. He spoke.

"You'll have to come back for another interview. Thank you Mister and Missus al-Habibi, you can go."

Emir's medical exam expired two weeks from our interview day, and the INS taking a deeper look into our lives would surely take longer than three weeks. A new medical exam would reveal Emir was carrying diseases that prevented immi-grants from being approved for green cards. And then there would be nothing we could do; he would be deported. It would end there, as another disaster, another foiled plan, another what-went-wrong.

We left the INS office in silence and walked back out onto the sidewalk. The city swam around me, a swarm of yellow cabs, dark suits, people warbling into cell phones, everybody rushing. The sky was coated in a thin cover of depressing gray clouds.

"We'll be fine," I said without thinking, to break the silence, the tension growing between us.

"Who will be fine?" Emir snapped. "Unless they come over and do their investigation and approve us within two weeks, which I seriously doubt, my medical exam will expire. Why did you have to stalk that Oliver?"

"It wasn't necessarily Oliver. We don't know who it was. Why did *you* date that meth-head Drew? *You* are why we have to worry about the medical test in the first place!"

Emir narrowed his eyes.

"I can't believe you would say that."

"It's the truth," I said.

"We came to New York because of you. If all that never happened with Oliver, I would have had my green card in L.A. last year! I wouldn't have met Drew and none of this would have happened."

"You don't know that. There's no way of predicting what's going to happen."

"But you can be smart. You can be smart in your life, and we have been idiots. Stupid. How did I ever let you convince me that getting married was a good idea?"

"It was. It is. We'll get through this."

"You are going to be fine. You always will be. *I*, on the other hand, am fucked."

We sat down on a bench outside a downtown office building and Emir stared into space, his face turned to stone. I wiped my eyes. Emir said he needed to be alone for a while. I said I understood. But he didn't go anywhere. I asked what he was thinking and he said he changed his mind because he didn't want to go throw himself off the Brooklyn Bridge. I said I thought the Brooklyn Bridge had fencing. Gary Kubiak. It wasn't Oliver who tried to turn us in; Oliver never found out I was the one who came across his LAPD page—he would have said something. Wouldn't he? The elimination of Oliver left me with only Julian as the culprit, but I didn't want to believe the former love of my life would have done that, no matter how bad things between us had become. I pushed the suspicion deep under. I should have been more prepared. Kubiak was sharp. He caught me by surprise. Had I expected some dumb, uninvested, uninterested, lazy bureaucrat?

I suppose I had.

It was exactly what I expected—to run through the machine. In and out.

Now there was no way back, no way out.

Instead of continuing to fight, we went to a dark bar in the middle of the day and ordered two Cosmopolitans.

What would we do? Emir and I had no idea. We could demonstrate plenty of evidence that we were not faking our love for his green card, but there was no way to fake the results of Emir's medical exam.

Only later would I remember that at some point during our friendship Emir had told me that all Muslim men are "cut." I could have had the right answer for Gary.

I thought I would remember this day as the day of our INS interview and that nothing else could intrude on this memory. I was covering the CEO's desk while his executive assistant went to a dentist appointment. I signed in to the computer and the interoffice instant messenger opened. I thumbed through an issue of *People* magazine that had come in on the last mail run. Then the computer beeped. A new instant message. From Oliver Fox?

He was newly hired in the L.A. office and saw my name on the IM list. He just wanted to say hello. Funny that we worked at the same company again.

*Yes, funny!* I replied.

That was all he had to say. I knew then he never found out what I'd done.

One of the summer interns, a redheaded college sophomore, came over to the desk and leaned over the marble counter. The intern startled me and I clicked Oliver off. The intern's eyes were glazed. He slurred his speech. I was the one who had the two-Cosmo lunch, what was wrong with this guy? He didn't smell of alcohol but it was obvious that something was off.

"Are you okay?" I asked.

Then he leaned in toward me as if to kiss me and I bolted back in my chair. I was relieved when he walked away. I reached for the phone to call Human Resources. He should be sent home for the day. But then I hesitated. He would be fired, his internship would be ruined, and it would probably do more damage than it was worth. I placed the phone gently back down on the receiver and turned back to *People* magazine.

Twenty minutes later, there was a commotion in the hallway. People from the other side of the floor were rushing around, looking confused, congregating outside the CEO's office.

"What's going on?" I asked an assistant.

"Someone jumped out a window. Twenty-second floor. We saw him fall."

*Saw him fall.* My mind flashed to images of bodies leaping from the World Trade Center two years earlier, how Emir had been there, how that day had led us here. The intern was off his medication or had recently started a new one, it wasn't clear which. I found out later that he had been going around to various offices, barging in on meetings, speaking incoherently. Eventually Human Resources was notified and he had been summoned to the office but he ran away, ducking into a freight elevator going up. He burst out on one of the highest floors, fought off a security guard, grabbed a chair, threw it out the window, and jumped out after it, crashing through the atrium of Remi, an upscale Italian restaurant twenty-two stories below.

I never expected the INS interview would be eclipsed as the strangest thing to occur that day.

An email circulated instructing us not to speak to the press about what was euphemistically dubbed "today's unfortunate incident." All employees were dismissed. I went downstairs, past the atrium where I got my morning coffee and overpriced frittatas. Police surrounded the restaurant. I did not want to see the sheet-draped body but I did, in the pedestrian walkway that served as the atrium of the restaurant. A wave of nausea washed over me. Powerful, overwhelming nausea. I crouched on the ground by the edge of the sidewalk.

# 14.

## Deus Ex

I wished I could have talked to my mother. This would serve my purposes twofold: it would be comforting to be able to turn to a parent—the only parent I had—and perhaps she could lend some practical advice. More than anything, I could not stand to upset her. I wondered what my father would have thought about all this. We traded occasional, infrequent letters that year. I'd written him one on William Morris stationery. He knew I was working for a famous entertainment company in New York. Beyond that, he was still shadowy, a living ghost.

All Emir and I could do was go through the motions, do as we were supposed to, for once, do as we were told. It was out of our hands now, and all we could do was hope we could prove what we needed to. It brought me back to my original question: how do you prove love? And the nature of that love? What were the boundaries of the type of love to be considered legitimate?

At home, we folded up my futon into a couch and pushed it out of my bedroom. We left my desk there and pushed Emir's desk from his bedroom into mine. There it was, the office I had told Fran the Broker we had wanted in the first place. We went back to work, living in a state of paranoia and fear. For three weeks, we heard nothing, and could only wait. Would Emir be deported? What would happen to me? It was difficult to fake that we were okay to the people we interacted with on a regular basis: bosses, colleagues, friends. We could not speak of it to anyone. This was the freedom to admit, for the first time, that some part of me had felt the marriage I idealized so much was some kind of a burden all along, that I had misshapen my memory of the previous two and a half years to make it seem like a wonderful escapade when I was wracked with worry about exactly what would happen. It *was* happening. Knowing things were bad released me from the worry that they would become bad. If we were already caught, we could no longer get caught.

We knew it was over when the medical exam was two days from expiring and we had still heard nothing. Emir mentioned he was considering going to Montreal to stay with El Toro and figuring it out from there. I wouldn't try to talk him out of it.

The next day, he was sitting at his computer as usual when he suddenly leapt from his desk chair, shouting, "What? No. No way! This can't be real!"

"What?" I asked.

"This email. It says I won the green card lottery."

"No!"

"Yes."

"That's absurd."

"Insane."

"Unbelievable."

"How?"

"Like everyone else who wins. At random."

"No way."

"Apparently, somehow, way."

It's a strange idea, the green card lottery. The United States Government decides we could use more immigrants from certain countries with a low influx of immigration to the States, and then these countries are listed in an eligibility section of a green card lottery website. If you are from one of the desired countries, you can enter. If you are among the (currently) one hundred thousand chosen via random computer-generated drawing (applications run in the millions), you receive the opportunity to apply for a green card. As long as you are determined not to be a potential terrorist or threat to national security, you get the green card. Aside from marriage to a citizen, the lottery is by far the easiest road to permanent resident status.

Emir entered every year, from when he was a freshman in college and even after he and I got married. After all, you never know. After Emir's diagnosis, after the INS interview, against all odds he finally won. The day he got the email, he ran around the apartment, cheering.

We talked about how in a movie or a novel, this would be the *deus ex machina* and virtually unbelievable, something conveniently contrived for the story. It would be a moment we would criticize—*I can't believe the screenwriters resorted to that*—except we couldn't do that, because this was our life. This happened.

I could not help but fantasize that the happy accident—the deus in the machina—was actually a blessing from my mother. That she had pulled some strings. Could she be behind it? Had she somehow manipulated the system from within? What if Emir's win was not random at all, but a gift from my mother? She was generous and kind and I feared her out of my own immaturity and inability to handle authority, but would she go as far as arranging something like this? I doubted such a thing could even be arranged but it was alarmingly coinciden-tal, given how hard it is to win the lottery; that Emir should get it now, when all hope was lost and we were struggling to figure out how to fight for him to stay in the country no matter what. For us to stay together.

*Your mom, the secret agent,* she would say with a dismissive wave of a hand. *Oh, please.*

I had a momentary fantasy that The Big Mom in the Sky had been keeping an eye on us the entire time, that she knew Emir and I had gotten married, and rather than confronting us or turning us in, she understood, and in fact had worked behind the scenes to help us along the way—our secret agent guardian angel. This, I knew, was wishful thinking. It's impossible to rig a DV lottery win and there was no way my mother wouldn't be angry and confrontational if she had found out.

Even the lottery win didn't guarantee that Emir would be granted the green card. His health conditions were still grounds for denial, but it would have been worse were he HIV-positive. Since we had brushed so closely against them,

I still thought about the consequences. The overturn of the U.S. law banning HIV-positive travelers and immigrant-hopefuls from entering the country was still six years in the future. Medical tests, which included an HIV test, were then still required for green card lottery winners: HIV-positive, no America. Emir's condition, too: if he had to take a new test, his status would be revealed and he would have to leave the country. Not even our marriage could save him then, not that it had done so well regardless. If he had to take a new exam, he would be better off forsaking the green card lottery altogether and trying to remain in the country illegally, the very thing we'd been trying to avoid for him in the first place.

There were no instant guarantees. The lottery win laid down the first bread crumb of a new trail; Emir still had to pursue it. Our case was becoming so complicated he hired another lawyer. The day he was slated to hear back from her about the case, Emir waited nervously, smoking and pacing through the apartment like a caged lion. When she finally called, she told him that they had until September 14th to finalize Emir's green card through the lottery before his medical exam expired and he would have to leave the country. Lottery win notwith-standing, his documents still needed to be reviewed, medical exam included. The green card would be granted pending that nothing suspicious turned up and that Emir was confirmed to be HIV-negative. If the INS hadn't processed all the paperwork by that date, Emir would have to take a new exam. And he wouldn't even bother; a new exam would mean no green card at all—ever.

I got home from work to find Emir frantically taking down posters and hiding his framed photographs of beach vacations with his male friends, pictures in which they mostly aren't wearing shirts and all have their arms around each other. I inhaled sharply, suddenly short of breath.

"Is Gary Kubiak coming over tonight?"

"No, sweetie, it's worse. My father has a business trip to New York. He just called. He gets here tomorrow afternoon and is coming over after checking into the hotel. I'm de-gaying the apartment."

I laughed at his phrase but was already grabbing the *Absolutely Fabulous* poster off the wall beside me.

"I thought it couldn't get worse than the INS. Here, let me help you."

We went from room to room, grabbing things left and right: Bette Midler movies, Barbara Streisand CDs, pictures from Pride Day in Boston when we were in a parade, and the AIDS Walk in Central Park. I peeled the NOBODY KNOWS I'M GAY magnet off of the refrigerator.

He put it into a large cardboard box with the other "gay things," and we then shoved the box beneath our five suitcases in the closet.

"Look, I'm in the closet again!" Emir said.

"I'm nervous about meeting my father-in-law," I said. "I don't want to mess this up."

"You haven't done something silly since that time with the

LAPD detective and the hot book thief. You've become a great wife. He will love you."

"What's the story these days, anything I need to have straight?"

"Just that I am."

"Obviously. But we still haven't fallen in love or anything?"

"No, I want to stay as close to the truth as possible, so that one day when I come out, if I ever do, it will be a shock instead of a major fucking shock. Actually, no matter what it will be a major fucking shock. Still, I'd like to keep the stories to a minimum."

The only pictures we left out on the shelves were our wedding photos, the ones Omar took, in which Emir and I are beaming in front of Elvis.

On Friday evening, Mohammad sat at our wobbly Ikea kitchen table. He wasn't at all tyrannical or as imposing a man as I had imagined. Mr. al-Habibi was attractive yet unassuming, of medium height and build. I could tell he had been handsome in his youth; he still was. He and Emir resembled each other in a similar way as I did my father: the aquiline nose, full lips, mega-watt smiles, and high cheekbones. He could have been my father.

"This is my dad," Emir said as I walked into the apartment after work.

Mohammad rose from the table. I reached out my hand to shake his, but he grabbed me, pulling me in to a tight hug.

"I am so happy to finally meet you, my new daughter," he said.

"Nice to meet you, too, Mr. al-Habibi," I said.

"You are so much more beautiful in person than you look in pictures."

"Thanks, Mr. al–Habibi."

"So, when are my grandsons coming?" he asked, affectionately patting me on the back.

I couldn't tell whether or not Mohammad was being serious.

"Don't bug her about that, Baba," Emir said.

"I could not believe after all this time the two of you are still not together. You look like a couple."

"Oh, we're not ready for a commitment that big yet. It's better to keep things this way, less pressure. We can just be husband and wife for the green card. I don't want to risk ruining our friendship," I said.

I felt my mouth curling up at the edges and was grateful Mohammad didn't know me well enough to recognize the sign I was lying. I thought of my mother's L.A. drop-in, how Emir and I were keeping the same secret in opposite ways from opposite-gender parents who would disapprove. But this was us, our decision, who we were—what would happen if we just laid it all out on the table? Wasn't the real enemy not immigration laws, not sexuality, not anything but secrecy itself?

"Come now. It's a wonderful favor you have done for my son. So generous," Mohammad continued. "But, you shouldn't feel confined by your reasons for marriage in the first place. Take it further, try to be together. I think you will find it won't ruin your friendship, but make it stronger. It has been a bit difficult for me to believe you would marry expecting nothing. No money, not a baby either? All young ladies want a baby. We had Emir's older sister when Yalda was a fresh bride, only twenty years old."

"Baba, things don't work that way here. Maybe in

Midwestern America but not in Los Angeles and New York City. We're focusing on our careers."

"Is it because you have a boyfriend and don't want to tell me that?" Mohammad asked.

For a moment, I thought he was asking Emir and I began to panic, but then I realized this boyfriend question was directed at me.

"Me? Oh, no. No boyfriend. Not these days. I've . . . gone on a few dates."

"And how do the young men feel about you being married?"

"Oh, you know. The more conservative guys don't really like it. An accountant and a British investment banker weren't fans. But artistic, bohemian men tend to be understanding."

"Like my son, who had to come all the way to America to become a bohemian."

"Baba, you are making this too complicated. Why don't we go for dinner?"

"Very fine then. I will get my jacket from your closet."

"I'll grab it, Mr. al-Habibi!" I said, and leapt up, bouncing over to the closet.

The "gay box" was way at the bottom, under the suitcases, but I would have rather been paranoid than taken any chances. I held out Mohammad's jacket.

"Emir, did you tell your wife of the surprise after dinner?"

Emir looked uncomfortable.

"What?" I asked.

"We're going . . . to a musical," Emir said.

"I got tickets for us already," Mohammad interjected. "I love Broadway. The show is tonight, you can come, right?"

"Definitely, Mr. al-Habibi, my plan was to spend time with you. What are we seeing?"

"*Beauty and the Beast*," said Mohammad. "And you needn't use formalities. Call me Baba."

"What's your favorite musical?" I asked, deflecting Mohammad's request.

"I don't get to see them very often as I am always traveling, but when I come to Manhattan and go to the Broadway and hear the musicals I find them artistic and beautiful. A favorite is difficult to choose but some years ago I saw one entitled *Cats* and I enjoyed this one very much."

First we went to dinner at Azalea, a restaurant around the corner from the theater. Talk of grandchildren seemed to have passed as Mohammad asked us about our jobs and about my mother.

"So your mother does the visa work and yet she is accepting of your relationship with my son?"

It was as if our presence at the same table had broken a dam; Mohammad began asking all the questions that had been bubbling up for almost a year by then.

"She doesn't know about the marriage," I replied between bites of pasta. I gulped from my glass of red wine.

"If she finds out and has a problem, you just tell her to call your Baba, and I will speak to her. Emir tells me she is apt to become—" Mohammad waved his hands around his head in a flailing manner "—easily upset."

"That she does," I said.

"She does indeed," Emir said.

I liked Mohammad. He made me miss my own father, the version of my father I knew from my earliest memories, when he played hide-and-seek with me after school. My father when he was joyous, when he laughed a lot.

My Father Before.

The kinds of memories that came back to me without warning were usually from After. On one of those summer Sundays, we decided to go to one of the beaches along Lake Washington. He met me in the hallway of his apartment building. His body swayed as we walked toward his front door to go into his apartment and pack our picnic. It was eleven in the morning and I knew he was drunk. I didn't know when he'd started drinking during the day, but that day I came to a full awareness of what my mother, my grandmother, and my father himself had been trying to conceal from me.

"Why are you looking at me like that?" he asked.

"I'm not," I said. I walked to the refrigerator, pulled out a Coke, cracked it open.

We took the bus to the lake. His license had been revoked (after a DUI, I later learned) and he never got a new one. He tried to hide it but I saw him pour vodka into the thermos. He made a display of pouring in juice as if that was all there was. I stared out over Lake Washington. Such a peaceful place. Sailboats, families on the sand, people splashing around in the water, a quiet, sunny day. My father was quiet, too. He lay on his back in the sun, his form reminding me of a beached whale, recalling my grandmother's refrain about him, *He was always a fish out of water.*

I sat between Mohammad and Emir at *Beauty and the Beast*, taking sideward glances at Baba-in-law, watching him watch the show. He smiled the entire time and during some songs his eyes went misty. A homophobe getting teary during a play based on a Disney cartoon? I wondered whether Mohammad was being this friendly because somewhere in his heart he knew, he just knew, that just as Beauty will end up with the Beast, his firstborn only son and I were destined to be together, that eventually we would get there, that—a tale as old as time, true as it can be, somebody bends, unexpectedly, just a little change, both a little scared, neither one prepared—love would find a way. My father would have cried at a musical, too.

Before he left for the airport, Mohammad asked if I thought there was any chance that I might be pregnant next year and I said we'd have to see.

In honor of Baba Mohammad's coming and going, Emir and I decided to resurrect our post-parental-visit drinks tradition, so I shook up a couple of dirty martinis over the kitchen sink.

"It's time for us to re-gay the apartment. We have to get you back out of the closet."

"I can't stand it for one more second in there."

"Are you sure Baba would be mad if he knew?" I asked, grabbing what Emir had begun referring to as "the box" out from underneath our five suitcases.

"Appearances deceive," he said.

Of course. We were doing the exact same thing.

I slapped the nobody knows i'm gay magnet back on the fridge.

15.

Final Interview

We were called for our follow-up interview. We brought our lawyer with us. We needed all the help we could get.

The office to which we were led was not Gary Kubiak's. It was decked out in full Ricky Martin regalia: Ricky Martin posters, Ricky Martin coffee mug, framed photograph of Ricky Martin. Magazine cutouts of Ricky Martin were everywhere around the office, and they were framed.

"They're fucking with us," Emir whispered.

Though it would be years until Ricky Martin came out of the closet, rumor already had it that he was gay.

"Someone just really loves Ricky Martin. I hope."

Then she walked in.

The woman who would decide our fate was Rubenesque, with long braids that were gold at the ends, as if they had been dipped in paint. She had the kind of fake nails that always made me wonder how women who got them managed to type or make a phone call. Large gold rings adorned her every finger and she was covered in shiny gold costume jewelry. She wore a candy-colored top over dark pink leggings, and what Emir referred to as "Dame Edna glasses." Her movements were slow and languid. She sat behind her desk, sizing us up and cocking a skeptical-looking eyebrow.

"Let's see'a file," she said in a thick Jamaican accent.

She could have been a Bob Marley backup singer. I wondered how she ended up here. Our lawyer handed over paperwork. The officer flipped through them, peering at some intently. I worried that the Ricky Martin pictures, gold braids, and air-brushed nails were a clever disguise for a top secret agent who could see through green card marriages just by looking at the couple.

"Yep, somet'ing not right," she said.

Emir looked pale. My forehead went clammy. *This is it. They know. She's on to us. They'll lead Emir away in handcuffs, I'll be carted off to prison, Emir will be deported, poor Lawyer will be disbarred—*

"What do you mean?" Lawyer asked, concerned but cool.

We had fooled the lawyer easily. This INS officer was a different story. She was smarter than she looked. My head pounded, hurting more than any hangover. I was frozen mid-breath and looked over at Emir. For someone so naturally expressive, he had a great poker face, but I recognized fear in his eyes.

"Where's the receipt?" Mrs. Ricky Martin asked.

"What receipt?" Emir, Lawyer, and I echoed in unison.

I flashed back to our wedding night, when the minister asked us for the marriage license and we had to put the wedding off to go downtown and get it. We were not organized. We should have been more on top of everything. What had we forgotten this time? I was still waiting for Mrs. Ricky Martin to open her mouth. *Why is she so slow? Why does she want to do this to us? I* knew it was on purpose, because the immigration police needed time to get down the hall with their guns and handcuffs. They were about to take us away, I could feel it in the seat of my soul. My intuition: it was never wrong. Except for when it was.

Then Mrs. Ricky Martin spoke.

"The receipt for the lottery."

"Lottery?" the lawyer asked, surprised. "That's not what we're here for."

Mrs. Ricky Martin was good. So inconspicuous. So skilled at holding us there as our lives were about to be ruined.

"No, this is for the lottery," Mrs. Ricky said.

"But the letter said to bring your spouse," said Emir.

"Yes, why did he receive this letter?" Lawyer jumped in, grabbing the letter and sticking it in the agent's face, pointing at the list of things to bring to the interview: *Spouse.*

Mrs. Ricky spoke. "He's been granted resident status by the diversity visa program and all he is missing is the receipt for the payment of the fee. And none of you should be complainin'— two chances at getting the green card is more than most people get. You are a lucky couple."

"All right then, can't Mr. al-Habibi pay the fee now and we can get this resolved today?" Lawyer asked.

"I'll have to go find my supervisor," Mrs. Ricky told us.

We sat for another half-hour until Mrs. Ricky returned, sans supervisor.

"I couldn't find him," she said. "We will have to postpone it. Come back with the receipt, and you can leave your wife at home."

I was like an object that didn't need to be in the room, a vacuum cleaner, a steak knife. After all our preparation, I was no longer a necessary component in Emir's green card–procuring process. It was shaping up to be a strange day indeed and I hadn't even had my coffee yet. We left the office frustrated that this was going to take more time, but a little bit relieved, too, that we no longer had to rely on our unconventional arrangement.

"We can fight it if they want you to take a new medical exam," Lawyer said.

"How can you fight about the medical exam?" I asked.

"They already broke the seal. It already counted. The INS screwed up by sending Emir the wrong letter. They should fix their mistake—and any little mistake should be *seriously* reviewed in this day and age. One little mistake and the wrong person could be in this country. We don't need any more intelligence errors, and that comes to when it negatively affects innocent applicants, too. Well, I'm off, kiddos. Emir, I'll be in touch about this as soon as I know anything more. Congrats on the lottery."

"Thanks, Lawyer," Emir and I echoed in unison.

Lawyer hailed a taxi, bound for his office and endless other immigration cases. Emir walked me to the other side of Broadway.

"Should I go into the office or should we go out and celebrate?"

"It's not even noon. We can have champagne tonight."

"It's a plan."

"Can you believe this good fortune? We don't even have to be married anymore," he said.

"But I don't think we should get divorced," I said. "Just in case. Something could still go wrong with your paperwork."

"I like being married to you, too, sweetie," Emir said, sticking out his hand to hail me a taxi. A yellow cab pulled over. "Wasn't she so blingy?" he continued, holding open the door as I got into the backseat. I hugged him.

Emir double-checked that both my legs were inside, and then he shut the cab door.

Emir withdrew the petition for the green card through marriage. The lottery had its own approval process, with the same agency, but Gary Kubiak was out of our lives forever. It was over. We had slipped through the looking glass. The old medical exam was accepted. Since it was used during the first interview, the lawyer got it through to the next even though the supposed expiration date had passed. Emir's residence in the United States was made permanent.

It didn't work out between Emir and a man from his therapy group, but he soon had a new prospect: Elevator Man. I'd heard about him before, the cute guy in the elevator at work. Elevator Man worked in an architecture office in the same building as the gay-porn-and-photography studio. Elevator Man was a blond, blue-eyed, teddy bearish, baby-faced architect from South Africa; that was all Emir knew about him. He didn't even know if the guy was gay: they'd only had brief, casual exchanges in the elevator, until Emir began timing his coffee break to coincide with Elevator Man's; and one day Elevator Man asked if Emir would like to join him, and Elevator Man became Stan.

After two dates, Emir told Stan about his health situation and prepared for Stan's interest to end there and then, but Stan didn't care. After that they became inseparable, Emir and Stan. EmirStan.

Emir and I were called for—of all things!—another interview. It was shaping up to be a recurring theme. This time, though, the interviewer was no INS special dispatch, but a young reporter from *Elle Girl* magazine.

This interview was different. I was nervous not because I feared we might be "found out," but because we were to make a full-scale confession, on the condition of anonymity. We had never told the whole true story on the record before. What would it feel like, I wondered, sitting across another table from another interviewer, on completely different terms? When we spoke of our emotional connection, would Emir and I agree that we were still as close, if not closer, than we were three years before? Did he have any regrets? Did I? When I look back on the strange and confusing decade that was my twenties, the time I spent married to Emir is still my fondest memory.

Which memory? All of it. The whole thing. The hardest moments had forced growth. And we were about to put it all down on record.

The interview was scheduled for six o'clock in the evening, on 53rd Street in Midtown, right down the block from the William Morris offices. Its finality lent it a feeling of urgency. I imagined the interview would be bittersweet, a graduation of sorts.

Emir waited for me outside my building when I got out of work. I had received good news; I was promoted to working for a literary agent, and a nice, young, laid-back one at that. My new boss was known as the guy you want to work for at William Morris, because he would never toss a stapler at you. It wasn't his nature. Emir congratulated me and we made our way down Fifty-Third Street to Maison, the French restaurant where we were to meet our interviewer.

"Are my lips white?"

He glanced at them.

"No."

"Good," I said. We arrived outside the restaurant. "Okay. I'm ready."

The reporter, a perky blonde twenty-five-year-old, was a friend of a friend of a friend who had heard about us. We reveled in being the gossip for a while, the surprise of the week, after those years of leading a double life. Word arrived to the young journalist as she was culling sources for a story about couples that married especially young and the reasons why they'd chosen to. When she called me she said she thought an immigration angle would perfectly round out her triad of young marrieds.

The three of us sat down at a candlelit table and ordered red wine and tap water that would later be charged to the journalist's expense account. The journalist placed her voice recorder on the table. *Tell me everything,* she said. Emir and I looked at each other, our faces lit up. *Who will start? Where should we begin?* We told all our favorite set pieces: how we met, the wedding night, our moments in the INS office, "saved by the scallop," and the green card lottery win. We cut each other off to add asides or tell the stories from the other perspective.

The journalist remarked that what I did was a generous, selfless act, that I had done something extraordinary for Emir by putting myself at risk of criminal prosecution, tens of thousands of dollars in fines, and jail time, to help him stay. I explained that I never saw it that way. I told her my selfishness theory, how I was afraid to be alone and all I wanted was to be with someone I loved who would not abandon me.

All of our stories had two versions, versions that were often quite different. As planned, STDs were left out, as was the brief love affair with methamphetamines. The journalist barely got her list of questions in edgewise, but she said we'd already answered them all.

Our story later appeared in an issue featuring Britney Spears on the cover—who had barely emerged from a fifty-five-hour stunt marriage, something she did when she was bored one night in Vegas. The piece was entitled "Why I Married So Young." The pull-quote, splayed across the middle of the page, is from me: "My ex-boyfriend couldn't accept that I married my gay best friend." I go on to say, "I know the marriage saved me from a bad relationship." I had been talking about Julian. To see these quotes taken from a much longer conversation stripped things down to a stark, simplistic truth.

When the issue came in the mail, I was eager to get a look at the two other couples the reporter had chosen besides Emir and me. One of the brides, from Houston, married because her boyfriend was in the Army and they'd been apart for three years. The other, from Phoenix, got pregnant at fifteen. Mine states I'm from Boston. Reason for marrying young: "I didn't want him to leave." It focuses on me more than Emir because the magazine is for girls and the girls want to know the girl's story, but also, as the journalist said, because it was obvious why he would marry me; he needed the green card. But I was the one who proposed to him, which she had some questions about. *You guys have a really special relationship*, the journalist said. *But let me get this straight—you were never in love with him?*

I'd heard this question before, and it once made me feel insulted, that I was perceived as that hopeless girl in love with her gay friend, as in *The Object of My Affection*. But over time I'd come to see it as funny and in some ways true. Yes, we were in love, a different kind of love. I loved him so much I felt as if I *should* have wanted to have sex with him—it would be so much more understandable in terms of how we fit relationships into neat categories, little boxes.

The other brides, in their photos, are in white and the grooms wear tuxedos. The white and blond army couple beams at the camera, and the Hispanic teen pregnancy twosome appear very serious. Emir and I look mysterious because we were photographed at home wearing paper bags over our heads. We had drawn faces on these paper bags, cartoon faces in Magic Marker.

The bag faces look pretty happy.

We knew we were coming to the end, and so we reminisced eagerly. *I use the story as a boyfriend filter. The guys who freak out aren't my type—I need an understanding guy who knows I was helping out a friend.* I was struck by the way the teen magazine portrayed us—they could have held us up as a scandal, as an example of what not to do, but instead the article placed us next to the other two couples in the same light, as another example of young marriage today, free of judgment. The teen magazine seemed to understand.

*Every girl should have a gay husband.*

The difference was in the images. We had paper bags on our heads and the other couples did not. The legality would remain in question. The army wife married because her boyfriend was being sent to work overseas, and the teen pregnancy husband married because, well, he impregnated a sixteen-year-old from a devout Catholic family. In some cases, getting married was just what you did. For us it was, too, but immigration and sexual orientation complicated the equation. The article's closing quote comes from me: "We're still best friends, but now it is time to move on."

I kept a copy of the magazine long after the pages turned yellow, and I have it still. I wonder if the army wife and teen mother did, too, the magazine stashed in drawers in Texas, Arizona, or wherever they have since gone. Are they still married? What happened to them? The page, divided into three columns, links us. When I look at it now, it is not to remind myself of my days with Emir—I don't need reminders for that—but of those two other couples who married for reasons very different, but as pointed and specific as my own. A teen pregnancy and a military career: each situation had somehow forced marriage or seemed to call for it, as the threat of Emir's deportation had for us.

Timing is a strange and interesting beast. The *Elle Girl* article, with my quote in it about how marriage to Emir saved me from a bad relationship, was still on newsstands when Julian came back. Again. We arranged to meet up at the bar of the Gramercy Park Hotel so that he could help me make some decisions about the 401(k) I had recently acquired from the agency. That was the reason, supposedly. We met in the dimly-lit lobby bar and ordered expensive drinks. I pulled out the 401(k) paperwork. We drank the overpriced cocktails and smiled a lot and he spent about two seconds deciphering my documents before we got down to real business—trying to figure out how and why we had failed as a couple. Were we doomed to failure? Neither of us thought so. We could never seem to get over each other, no matter who else we saw, how hard we tried, etc.

My negative feelings, now captured forever in the print archives of *Elle Girl*, dissolved and I turned right back into that love-struck sixteen-year-old. He had that power over me. Since Emir had turned me into another ardent *Sex and the City* fan, I'd taken to thinking of Julian as my Mr. Big. Carrie was a writer, too, and Big, a powerful businessman. Only she had great shoes, a perfect body, and witticisms for any situation. Julian, like Mr. Big, was the one who got away, but sometimes reappeared when least expected. Julian and I were definitely no Carrie and Big, but glamorizing us via these fantasy, larger-than-life archetypes made it easier to imagine us finding a happy ending.

We moved back toward each other slowly this time, seeing each other, emailing, and talking on the phone. Maybe we would end up as friends. After the broken engagement and the betrayals, friendship, I thought, was safer. When Julian emailed me a surprise, a plane ticket receipt to accompany him to Puerto Rico for a weekend getaway, I told him I would go on the condition we could go as friends, and he agreed. For two days we shared a bed and did not make love. We hardly touched at all except for one night when we took our doubly left-footed selves to a salsa club, and by the end of the weekend all I wanted to do was grab him around the waist. He made me feel protected and secure. We spent the whole plane ride back to New York kissing. He missed me so much, he said. He was sorry our engagement broke up, and especially about the way it did—that we stopped talking. So was I, I told him, deciding I was a different person then, an immature person who made stupid mistakes without regard for consequences. Maybe I still was, but the sequence of events brought me where I needed to be—with Emir—and now I was ready to spend the rest of my life with Julian, just as I had initially predicted.

Julian had moved from Park Slope back to Manhattan and lived two blocks away from my office, in a high-rise on West

53rd Street. I moved some suitcases full of clothing over there. Emir was understandably skeptical but said if I was happy then he was happy for me. Julian and I were officially back together.

"Are you still married?" he asked.

"Yes," I said, afraid I was in for it again, but then he said something that erased any lingering fear I had about his reaction to my being married to Emir.

"Well, what if I want to marry you? What happens then?"

"You might still want to?"

"Well, we can't consider it as long as this situation is in effect."

"Emir already has his green card." I explained that, in the end, he didn't get it through me, that he'd won the lottery.

"He won the green card lottery? How lucky is this bastard?"

"It was very lucky."

I didn't mention exactly how lucky it really was, or why.

"So you don't have to be married to him anymore?" Julian asked. "Why didn't you get divorced?"

I shrugged. "Hasn't been a reason yet."

Emir and I, both in serious relationships, were moving on, though it would take more time before either of us was willing to admit it. Later he would tell me, "I was sad because I felt like things were changing and we were both starting our own lives. It had to happen sometime though, or we would have become each other's comfort bubble." He may as well have been explaining my own feelings back to me.

At the same time, my mother and I came up with a plan to

invest in a small apartment in New York; she would cover the down payment and I, the mortgage and monthly maintenance. I started looking around.

"It's going to have to be soon and I know it will turn out fine but I dread telling him this chapter is coming to an end. We've been such close friends for so long now. I guess it can't really change that, but it's that I've gotten used to him," I wrote in a journal. How often does having "gotten used to" someone keep us in relationships long after it's time to move on?

Emir knew that when I found something I would be moving out, and yet neither of us believed it was really going to happen. I spent months doing research for my mother's investment, so it seemed a long way off anyway.

Until it wasn't.

A tiny one-bedroom third-floor walk-up co-op apartment in Chelsea was within our price range. The living room window looked out into a garden and the sound of birdcalls, not traffic, filled the space when the windows were open. It was a ten-minute walk from Uncle Vance's loft. I was leaving my gay husband to move to Chelsea.

It was a lovely sort of anchor.

We put in an offer on the apartment that afternoon and it was accepted the following day. Then only one more step stood between my mother and me and the beautiful apartment: an interview. In New York City, co-ops are operated by notoriously strict boards. The board has to approve new tenants, make sure they are desirable candidates for the building. It is an extensive review process: all conceivable documents and records are examined, including employment history, tax returns, letters of recommendation. If they required photo albums, it would have been the INS all over again.

At home, I pored through Emir's careful filing system that held all of our records, grateful that one of us was so organized. I hoarded memorabilia down to restaurant matchbooks and airplane wine bottles, but bureaucratic documentation I hated. I threw away credit card statements, bank statements, and would probably have chucked my tax returns if it wasn't for Emir. The co-op board had asked for the past three years' worth of returns. That was as long as I'd been a taxpayer. I pulled them out and made copies at the mailbox place down the street, and then put them in with the rest of the paperwork comprising my application packet. I made three copies of the whole packet, put them in folders, and they were ready to go.

Except there was a bit of a problem.

If my mother saw my tax returns, and she would see them since we had to assemble the board package together, it was inevitable that she would find out Emir and I were married. After everything, the IRS—not INS—threatened to out me to my mother as Emir's bride. I could either come up with an excuse to back out of closing on the apartment so as not to let this happen, or come out and tell her the truth. If I said nothing, went ahead with the closing, my mother would notice Emir's name along with mine on the tax returns. She would carefully review all the documents with a Visa Chief's scrutiny. There was no way I could hide. Since Emir won the visa lottery the only consequence I faced was my mother's disappointment and anger. The news of my marriage would feel like a slap in the face, a complete disregard for the career that won her multiple awards, promotions, and raises, the career that allowed her to raise me. It didn't get any closer to biting the hand that feeds you—my mother's job had kept us afloat for all those years she was a single parent.

I wondered if my mother's own initial deception of her parents when she married my father would help her understand that when you want something enough nothing can stop you from doing it. More likely she would not perceive any similarity between our marriages. Hers was "real," after all. I began to think about what I would say. This was my chance at honesty with my mother. I could explain that I had married Emir out of love, even if it wasn't what we think of as the traditional kind that leads a couple to wed. I could tell her about Emir, how I didn't want him to face the consequences: being gay in a place where that was dangerous. I would explain that compassion was a value she taught me, that she taught me to think of others and consider them when making decisions. *Always be nice to people,* she advised. I had done what I could both to help Emir and to keep him with me because he was my friend and I loved him. Our relationship was special and Emir, special enough to marry. How does it get more real than that?

I stayed late at work, sitting at an empty desk and staring down the phone. It was time to let her know what she so easily could have found out all along. There was something she was going to find out if I didn't tell her myself, I said. It would come up in the board meeting, perhaps, where she would be teleconferenced in, or she would see it on my tax returns. I explained, trying to keep my voice steady, even, and calm, I had gone to

Las Vegas with Emir in November of 2001 and, while we were there, we got married.

"HOW COULD YOU DO THIS TO ME?" Her voice boomed through the receiver. Assistants a few rows away from me turned around. My mother had not found out on her own. The lottery win was random. She'd had nothing to do with it.

"It's not something I did to you," I said. "I did it for Emir, and for me."

"But why? Why would you?"

"I had to. I needed him to stay."

"You married Emir for his *green card!?*"

"I thought you assumed."

"You could be arrested!"

"It's over now. He won the green card lottery."

"I'm going to check on that. You better not be lying."

"I'm not. I'm done with lying."

"Oh, Lize! Marriage is a sacred bond. Lize!"

"Emir and I have one. And please stop calling me—"

"But it's not a marriage!"

"—Lize."

"Marriage is a social institution and when you marry you agree to certain rules society has set."

"Rules change, or at least they need to. It used to be a business transaction, an arrangement. Interracial marriage used to be illegal the way gay marriage is now."

"You cheated the system."

"The system was cheating him."

"You can annul it."

"I would never!"

My mother sighed on the other end of the phone.

"If you love him so much," she said, "then why are you leaving him for an apartment?"

My mother's question floored me; I didn't yet know the answer. Had I learned the valuable marriage lessons I thought I'd set out to learn going into this? No, there were no lessons. That in itself was the lesson. There is no road map for marriage. There is no such thing as a test run. I never would have that model, what I initially thought I lacked from my parents. Every union was unique and individual, you just go into it and hope for the best and take things as they come. I had learned there was nothing I was going to learn that would help me with any relationship other than the one I was in.

"Lize?"

"I don't know."

"You don't? It's obvious. It's what happens in a lot of marriages."

"What?"

"You outgrew each other. It doesn't work anymore and it's time to move on."

"Like you and my father?"

She, too, had been the one to make the decision that she didn't want to be with him anymore. She'd once said, when I asked her about the decision to divorce rather than work on the marriage, that "there's nothing to work on when you don't want to be with someone anymore."

And she was right.

As with most of our talk about the past, the comment went unacknowledged.

"We'll move ahead with the closing when you show me your divorce papers."

Emir sat in the black rolling office chair at the desk in his bedroom, watching a black-and-white samurai film. I rapped lightly on the French doors and he gestured for me to come in. Emir took his headphones off. I sat on the edge of his bed.

"Honey," I said. "I have to make a decision. My mother knows we're married now, and if we don't get a divorce, I'll lose the apartment."

He spun around.

"How did she find out?" he asked, sounding panicked.

"I told her."

"YOU told her?"

This was shaping up to be the day when I turned out to have done the very things the two people closest to me did not want me to do.

"She was going to find out! She would see my tax returns in the co-op application."

"And you didn't think of this before you decided to let her buy a co-op with your name attached?"

"I had no idea they were going to need so many documents!"

"Is she going to try to deport me?"

"No, she isn't. She wouldn't do that to you. Us."

He looked at me skeptically.

"I'm her daughter and you're my best friend. We're safe."

Still, Emir was so nervous that he called her. He felt he owed her an explanation now that I had told her, that his voice needed to be heard or else he was exactly what she thought he was. He told her it was true that I had offered, and we'd gone back and forth about it, weighing the risks and possible consequences. That he had tried everything else and time ran out and she should know that her daughter was generous above all else. She listened. She wanted to know why we didn't come to her, ask for her help, because maybe she could have aided an asylum bid. As Emir wanted financial independence from Mohammad, I needed to break away, emotionally, from my mother.

Emir and I were both moving on, and if we didn't go our separate ways, we might actually end up staying "together" forever. It was so normal, this life. It would be hard to change, but change felt necessary. He agreed to the divorce; he said he was grateful I stayed married to him until his permanent green card came through via the lottery. I felt as if I was being asked to choose between my mother and Emir, instead of between one living situation and another. It was Emir's calm about it, his sweetness, that made it hard to decide what I really wanted, but the journey of growing up and moving on won out. I thought I had been independent from a young age, yet in a sense I hadn't been so at all.

Emir said he understood. "We could go on, but then we'd be forty-five living together. You'd be my hag, I'd be your fag."

We laughed at this but the truth was, this vision made us both a little nervous. When we did settle down, we'd learned, we wanted the passion, engulfment, and entanglement of relationships based on mutual physical attraction. We were both turning out to be more traditional than either of us thought we were. Our marriage was right for a time, and I wondered if entering a marriage you know will be good for you for some foreseeable future—but not "forever"—could be a justifiable act. At least you're well aware of your odds for divorce. It doesn't come as a life-shattering surprise. As a child of divorce, it helped assuage my fear of it.

I remembered back to the night in Los Angeles when Emir and I watched *The Object of My Affection*. How the Nina character falls in love with George, and when she decides to have a baby on her own, she initially hopes George will raise the child with her.

Emir satisfied my emotional needs, my need for another who listened and understood and offered unconditional love and support. It was a cozy place where I was welcome to stay, but I also suspected it was dangerous to try to separate love from sex for a marriage: in the movie, when Nina asks her step-sister how long it's been since she had sex with her husband, and Nina takes the blank look of a response to answer the question of whether all partnerships, marriages, long-term relationships turn to friendship in the end. All common wisdom and psychology magazine advice dictated that relationships built on sexual attraction rather than friendship fizzle as the initial chemistry becomes familiar, that unless there is enough of a friendship, with common interests, lifestyles, and goals, the partnership cannot be sustained. If I didn't take this opportunity to move on from the life Emir and I shared, there was a chance I never would. I would choose to have boyfriends, but where could these relationships go if I was already married?

Even if I continued being married to Emir until I got re-engaged to the great, straight love of my life, I would still miss

the opportunity to live alone as an independent adult, supporting myself financially and emotionally, growing responsible as
I grew further away from the headstrong girl who had married
her best friend to keep him with her. This stage could not be
skipped. Relationships had been about need and desperation.
Ever since I'd been able to see it I wanted to break free of it, so
that when I next encountered love it would not be about des-
perate need, a desire to be saved, or the opposite—the desire
to save somebody else. Turned out I'd been seeking salvation
from nothingness.

The apartment in Chelsea was large the way four hundred
square feet can seem large when you live in New York City. It
was large compared to the home Emir and I shared. I would
have space and time to myself, and Julian and I would have a
place where we could be alone. It felt both incredibly freakish
and totally right, given my life's trajectory, to have ended up
back together with my high school love, the man I had called
my soul mate when I was sixteen and still believed in such
things. Maybe I could again.

I called my mother and told her Emir and I would be
divorced by the time we were to close on the Chelsea apartment. I was putting a new life into motion. Everything was
changing again. This time I knew I was ready. If I offered my
hand in marriage to Emir for the green card, I also did it to
create a sort of blanket to shelter me from the loneliness I felt
in my early twenties, a feeling that intensified over the course

of that first year in L.A.

I asked Emir if he wanted help finding someone to take my room but he knew of someone who was looking for one in New York: Emma, of the Em & Em days. My stomach sank in spite of myself as I felt that familiar old twinge of envy. I felt this even though I'd been the one who wanted to move out. Emma wasn't taking my place; Emir was with Stan and I was with Julian. Our relationship with each other couldn't remain center stage. It was what happens in many close relationships: though we were still great friends, we had grown apart.

In early attempts at telling this story, I got caught up in how the marriage made our relationship into what it would become. This was thinking backwards. I wondered whether I had been preoccupied with the wrong question all along, whether or not the marriage was legitimate if the motivating love was non-sexual. Maybe the fact that a marriage proposal was my initial reaction to Emir's possible deportation was answer enough. Feelings between us that already existed let the words *I'll marry you* spill from my mouth without a pause to consider the pact we would be entering into. If our connection weren't natu-rally special, if I hadn't already known on some level that our compatibility would ferry us through any challenges marriage brought our way, it wouldn't have occurred to me to ask. That my reaction to his possible deportation was to propose said more about our relationship than anything else I could say in an attempt to define us, explain our friendship, or show how close we were. Keeping him with me was worth any risk. Whatever, in the end, that might have been.

## 16.

## Happy Divorce, Honey . . .

*DIVORCE. $499.*

Add a decimal—*$4.99*—and it could have been a hamburger. We didn't want to do it that way. We wanted to do it, as with our plan for everything all along, in partnership, a plan that had succeeded and failed at many junctures along the way. Emir's friend Wesley, a tax attorney, took on our case pro bono. Wesley had no experience in matrimonial law, but in our case none was needed. Divorce lawyers wouldn't have appreciated us as clientele. With no joint property, no alimony, no children, and as an agreeable, amicable couple, we were the divorce industry's nightmare—minimal billable hours. And divorce, like marriage in this country, is an industry.

Contrary to my initial expectation, I did get sad. I was a person who synchronized easily. Emir was home and family and now we were separating, breaking it up. If our marriage was not a marriage, why did the divorce—my light divorce, my happy divorce—upset me so? Given my reaction to the prospect of his departure three years prior, I suppose I shouldn't have been surprised.

Emir brought the initial round of forms home from Wesley's office. I opened a bag of barbecue potato chips and Emir rolled a joint. We looked through the paperwork together as we smoked. There were far more documents involved in getting divorced than getting married, and they were filled with legal jargon. Choosing a reason was the final piece of this puzzle that came together to tell the story of our weird marriage. New York was one of the few remaining fault states at the time; to obtain a divorce we had to decide on some grounds—"irreconcilable differences" was not an option.

Wesley had mentioned that the most common reason women plaintiffs cite is "mental cruelty," but I shunned that one. It was the most dishonest reason. This seemed a strange thing to care about given the circumstances of our marriage but I wanted our paperwork to reflect my true feelings, and Emir was never cruel to me. I doubted he was capable of being cruel. Bitchy, yes, maybe, but never cruel.

We smoked the joint and finished the chips, but still didn't have our reason. Emir brought in a bag of microwave popcorn and we devoured that, too.

Adultery. Abandonment. Imprisonment of three consecutive years or more.

No, no, and thank God no.

Emir flopped down on his bed, by the window, where he could smoke a cigarette. "What else is on the menu, sweetie?"

"Alcoholism . . . drug addiction . . . criminal conviction . . . If we want to be honest, we're really coming up short here."

"What about 'he was gay and I knew it all along but still I couldn't stand to lose him and he was going to be deported so I married him and then he won the green card lottery and we stayed married for another year because we love each other and we like our marriage but now my mother has bought an apartment in Chelsea and I want to live there and so I am leaving him.'"

"Oh, yeah. How did I miss that one? It's right here. Check. Done."

"I guess we should just choose something. It doesn't *really* matter."

Emir stubbed out his cigarette and returned to the desk.

"What about this one?" he asked, peering over my shoulder.

"Neglect?"

"Failure to perform in conjugal duties."

"Oh my God. It's perfect."

"That's why you couldn't tell Gary Kubiak that I was circumcised. You hadn't seen it in so long, you forgot."

I played the Doors song "The End" as we finished up the paperwork: checking boxes, signing on dotted lines, etc. It was that old film school training: think about how sound influences emotion and mood in a scene, how the right music can intensify the intended effect, while the wrong music could render it silly or ironic.

I remembered *The Junky's Christmas*, how Emir and I were picking out music when we got the bad news that the film could not be processed. I remembered the front page of the script and how it was the first time our names were linked on paper. I remembered each subsequent time: marriage certificate, bank statements, bills, leases, immigration papers. The divorce would be an end to the recording of our lives with such precision and accuracy. The mission was over.

Things left behind when I moved out:

> nobody knows i'm gay magnet, Amsterdam row house magnets, rolling wardrobe rack, framed photos of us on "dates," our entire INS photo album.

I would miss these things but at the same time couldn't bear to take them with me. They belonged with Emir.

The interior of the courthouse downtown, where we went to file the papers, strangely resembled the marriage license office in Las Vegas. Instead of excited anticipation this room was filled with grief. Women cried, men looked worn-out and bedraggled, and babies screamed. These were people at their wits' end. Emir and I were going about our day. Being surrounded by real suffering and heartbreak reminded us of how lucky we were. Our divorce was not an ending. Though our relationship would change, it would not dissolve.

Emir made life feel heightened in a time of circular, repetitive days of coffee-mailroom-happy hour-home. I had a larger mission, a sense of purpose when I felt I had none. The day-to-day of it all held as many long mundane stretches as adventures, but we were also engaged in a kind of dance of documents, records, of stepping outside of direct experience to take stock of it all—all the tracking and photographing and gathering of documents was satisfying. I felt proud of our files, our albums, our evidence, the accumulation of it all, the ongoing process of becoming. I wondered what kind of shape we would be in next.

Emir had his green card, mission accomplished—in the end it had everything to do with luck and nothing to do with me, though if I hadn't married him, he might not have been here to win. When I moved out, Emir helped carry boxes down the six flights of stairs, just as we had carried them up over a year before.

In time, I inched back toward the belief I'd started with, that our marriage deserved to be treated as authentic, even though it also was exactly as it appeared on the surface: a green card marriage with my best friend. But I no longer saw it as black-and-white, one or the other. We occupied a gray area where there was no simple explanation—any I had ever tried to give felt wrong. We'd been less than lovers, but being married changed the nature of our friendship. It wasn't friendship anymore; we could never be just friends. We'd never sleep together either. We had transformed into something else, something more than siblings, different from lovers. Though we were divorced on paper, he was still husband number one. I thought of the answer I gave the *Elle Girl* magazine reporter when she asked a question she was embarrassed to ask yet had no choice but to ask.

Yes, I had told her. Yes, yes, I'd been in love with him. Still was.

Part IV:
# 'Til Death or the Department of Homeland Security Do You Part

## 17.

## Aftermath

When my divorce from Emir was finalized, Julian and I got re-engaged despite my having called him the wrong man in print in *Elle Girl* magazine. This put me on the third engagement of my twenties, and I wasn't even halfway through the decade yet. A strange fact was that Julian did the same thing with the proposal as the first time, but this time he went even further. He slipped the next ring, a bigger ring than the last one, on my finger during the night while I was fast asleep. Unconscious. I woke up in the morning, and there it was. I wondered if it was a deliberate move, or if he had forgotten that this was how he did it before. We were back here again. *I was right, in the end,* I thought, remembering the way I looked at our relationship as an adolescent, that it was destiny, we were simply meant to be together. *He was the right person . . . that was just the wrong time.* It was the very definition of having my cake and eating it too: I'd helped Emir and would get to marry Julian after all. Here was proof! *The universe does reward good deeds! Karma is real!*

I abandoned my initial concept—that any man who disapproved of or didn't understand the nature of my marriage to Emir was not the man for me—in wanting to marry Julian. He hated that I'd married Emir so soon after our own engagement ended; though he knew that the love Emir and I shared wasn't sexual, that didn't stop the jealousy. Julian was possessive. I chose to interpret it as a sign of how much he loved me. We had been engaged before and he'd known me longer than anyone else. Julian, then, was not someone who would be disqualified for being ideologically, morally, or politically against my marriage to Emir. The stakes for Julian were personal, so it was easy to break my own self-imposed rule.

Julian and I finally made it to the altar. We went twice, as if to make up for the lack of a wedding three years before.

Emir was the witness at my second wedding, though not officially on paper as he was supposed to be. At the last minute, Julian got a friend of his to come to City Hall in lower Manhattan with us, too, because Julian was afraid that Emir's name on the witness line might come across as suspicious in our INS interview—a foreign ex-husband acting as witness at his former wife's next wedding was not normal, would not look good to the INS in Julian's case.

He would be getting his green card through marriage to me, too. Even though Julian and I were getting married out of love—straight, sexual, "traditional" love—our first wedding, the fast, official one at City Hall, was because of Julian's suddenly troubled visa situation. This was synchronous and accidental, that Julian happened to be Mexican and Swiss and not a U.S. citizen. We got engaged again at the end of the summer of 2004, ten months between my marriages. I thought of how I'd told Jen and Kate that Julian and I were going to wait until I was twenty-four to get married. In the end, that was exactly what happened, and though it wasn't anything like what we'd planned, my sense of destiny about the whole thing was back.

That Julian, high school boyfriend, first fiancé, became my second husband was absurd enough to make complete sense. At sixteen I had insisted—both to myself and to my mother—that he was THE ONE. At nineteen, the year I met Emir, I'd written in a journal, about Julian: "When you marry me, we will know: so there isn't this thing called fate? But maybe life introduced us early so we could grow apart and arrive back around again—a great big elevated circle . . . I see you, through years of distance, resentment, and a certain nonspecific longing in some remote corner of my being—only knowing it had to do with you." (But did it? The same words could have applied to another man who was consistent only in his absence.)

In terms of the green card thing, it was as if the universe were playing some kind of funny joke. And I was in on it. This time, I was laughing, too.

"Only you, sweetie," Emir said.

The lawyers at Julian's investment bank made a paperwork mistake that could possibly cost Julian his H-1B. Until it was sorted out, he could work from the London office. Not wanting to uproot when I had finally found stability in New York, I told him that since we were already engaged—a beautiful diamond on my ring finger—we could simply marry sooner than we planned; our ceremony was set for July 2005. We would be married by a Mayan shaman on a Mexican beach, in the country where we met, in a language we did not understand—a dead language. Since the Mayan ceremony was not legally binding, the plan was first to officially marry in Manhattan's City Hall. Instead of waiting until the summer, we could go ahead with it then, in November 2004, and leave everything as planned for our symbolic ceremony in July.

Because I feared she would be upset at the suddenness of the ceremony and her inability to be there, I did not tell my mother.

I was secretly married again, perhaps only out of habit. There was no reason to keep the City Hall union a secret from anyone, but we did. Maybe I was afraid it would make the July ceremony in Mexico feel less real.

A few days later, we left to spend Thanksgiving at my grand-mother's house in Seattle, just the three of us. My grandmother loved Julian. She treated him like a grandson, and the affection was mutual. At dinner, after a thimbleful too many of red wine, my grandmother told me there were some things about my father I didn't know, but probably should. It had been six years since it happened.

"Since what happened?" I asked.

Julian sat beside me at the table. He said nothing. My grand-mother put down her fork and told the story confirming my suspicion that my father hadn't simply decided to cut off contact with me, that something had gone very wrong.

The year I was a freshman in college, my grandmother ran into a family friend on the street. He told her he was worried; he had run into Giovanni, and he was homeless. My father had been evicted from his apartment that year. His drinking out of control, he showed up drunk for work at the restaurant or stopped showing up at all. Whether he quit or was fired, I don't know, but the family friend told my grandmother that he had found my father living in Volunteer Park. Volunteer Park was down the street from my father's old apartment. We used to go for long walks there, through the greenhouse and around the footpaths. My grandmother called my grandfather, who drove from his second wife's house to meet her at the park. There, they found my father lying on the grass, his ankles swollen, toenails grown long, and clothing tattered.

My father took to the bottle and the streets. It was hard to picture. I kept repeating it to myself in an effort to understand, to help reality sink in, to feel its weight. Still it was as if I never fully could, as if it were someone else's story. The Italian gentleman I'd hardly known was a man who dressed elegantly in cashmere sweaters and suit pants, who donned a cravat on occasion, who combed his thick, dark hair so it would wave just so, who sprayed light, spice-scented aftershave on his smooth tanned skin; it was hard to reconcile with the image of a drunken man sleeping on the ground, the type of man I would never be able to look at with indifference again. From then on, when I saw a homeless person, it felt personal. I thought of him. Was he the type who had a shopping cart stuffed to the brim with whatever he salvaged of his belongings, and random paraphernalia collected off the streets? Did he have a cup for change? If he had no money, how did he get his alcohol? Was he a loner as he had been before; or to cope with living outside in the elements and having to survive, did he band together with other members of Capitol Hill's homeless? Did he have "drinking buddies," or was he alone? I had so many questions no one could answer. No one but him, and I wouldn't ask him these things because I didn't want to cause him shame.

My grandparents tried to coax him from the park but he wouldn't go with them. My grandmother told my mother, who said never to tell me. My mother was trying to protect me, the same way I later tried to protect her by telling her nothing about Emir.

After a few more tries, my grandparents succeeded in getting my father off the ground and to the hospital, where he was treated for alcoholic liver disease. They bought him a plane ticket back to Italy. My father was in his sixties and back living with his mother. He had gone to America and had a reverse experience of the immigrant dream. He had lost everything.

My grandmother told me that when they took him to the airport he was "sitting there like a prince." I did not know what that meant and yet I could imagine. Then she reminded me of another memory of which I have no recollection: when I was fifteen or sixteen, visiting for the summer, I went with some friends to surprise my father at his apartment. I had returned to my grandmother's house upset because I'd found him drunk. I can't remember this at all, but I know it must be true.

"My mother, why didn't she tell me?" I asked that night at the Thanksgiving table, already grateful that my grandmother had. I asked even though I already knew.

"She wanted to keep it from you," my grandmother said, "because she didn't want you to get hurt."

The impulse to shelter by withholding potentially painful or disappointing information was one I understood. I had done the same thing to her when I married Emir. Among the reasons I didn't tell her was that knowing would hurt her. We can pretend that certain truths don't exist—for as long as we can keep up the act.

At the beach ceremony in Mexico in July of 2005, Emir walked me down the aisle of sand—if I was anyone's to "give away" I was his.

Julian and I got to work setting up house in the little apartment in Chelsea. We split a cab to work in the morning, both of us in our business suits. He kissed me good-bye at 48th and 6th and I continued up to 53rd Street. At night, we lay on the blue sectional couch in the living room and watched movies on the big flat-screen TV. I was in heaven. I was married, again. A marriage with sex, and plans for babies down the line. (Way down the line, Julian and I agreed.) Julian, a romantic, took me out for date nights regularly. We went to our local sushi restaurant in Chelsea and fancier places the other direction down 15th Street, in the Meatpacking District. Julian liked to stay in hotels, and one night, to celebrate a successful merger of some sort (I never understood the Wall Street stuff), he booked a room at the Hotel Gansevoort. It was a few blocks away from the apartment and I thought it was a little overindulgent but I said nothing, and we went out dancing at Cielo with his finance friends. Bottles and bottles of champagne and top-shelf vodka arrived at the tables they roped off for us. I had stepped into the life of Carrie in *Sex and the City*. After a long struggle of an on-and-off relationship, I had landed my own Mr. Big.

Julian was also supportive of the dream that I was reluctant to admit to anyone but that I wanted more than anything: to be a writer. Writing was how I processed and understood the world around me. Joan Didion put it best when she said, "I write entirely to find out what I'm thinking." In a chaotic childhood and adolescence, it was something I could shape and control. Since Julian was doing well financially and I didn't have to rely solely on my minimal assistant's salary at the agency, I could afford to take some writing classes.

Working for the literary agent, I understood the business side of the publishing industry, the hundreds of revisions a manuscript went through before editors even saw it (I had assumed writers were geniuses who produced exactly what was in the published book on the first draft), and all the hands that went into making a book. I had learned about authors building their careers by writing for glossy magazines and websites. I had even landed a couple of assignments myself, writing some installations of a Nerve.com column called "Sex Advice From . . ." The column consisted of interviewing people in various professions (sushi chefs, personal trainers, corporate lawyers) to get their best sex and love tips. My boss represented Nerve.com for their coffee-table sex books. I spoke on the phone with the "Sex Advice From . . ." editor regularly. One day, I pitched her "Sex Advice from Diplomats," because I knew my mother would do anything for my success, and that Nerve.com was unlikely to get this particular query from anyone else.

It was a little start, but it was a start and my first byline. Having a byline was addictive. I wanted more. Unlike Tina, that turned out to be a good thing. I attended my writing classes faithfully, churning out draft after draft of every story and essay I wrote. Some were unsalvageable failures. Others surprised me and worked. The first piece accepted for publication was at the height of the San Francisco gay marriage boom. It was a personal essay about Emir and me, and the editor of the "Modern Love" column in *The New York Times* wanted to run it.

I told Julian when he got home that night, expecting he would be as thrilled as I was.

"You can't publish that," he said.

I was dismayed. Julian didn't want the essay out there. Understandably he feared an investigation about our marriage—as he was also getting his green card and it could look as if I was an alien smuggler, just as my mother said. But I cleared the essay with a publishing lawyer and assured Julian it would not jeopardize him as the marriage with Emir was portrayed as it was to me—real. Emir said that as long as a lawyer had signed off on it, congratulations on breaking into the *Times*.

With Julian, I had no such luck.

"You can't publish it," he insisted. "I'll be so embarrassed and harassed at work if my colleagues find out my wife was married to a gay guy."

"What? You would sabotage my chance to break into *The New York Times* because some assholes at work might make fun of you? I doubt those bankers even read the Styles section."

"Their wives do."

There was no convincing him. I let it go. When the essay came out, I did not tell him. He found out a week later when it was open on his former roommate's coffee table. When Julian was over visiting, he told Julian to tell his wife congratulations on the great article.

"How could you do this to me?" Julian boomed when he came home. "I can never trust you again."

It was so similar to what my mother said when I confessed I had married Emir. My marriage to Emir let down two of the most important people in my life, but still I stood behind it and believed in what I'd done. I cried and begged for Julian to forgive me, even though the publishing lawyer was right and the article brought no negative consequences. No one at work gave Julian any trouble about it. It was, in the end, just one woman's love story. The first year of marriage to Julian, though, began growing difficult, the fights becoming as frequent as the blissful times. He blamed work stress as the reason why he came home in a rage. He hated my cooking, I couldn't keep the apartment tidy enough, and I was failing in my role as wife. I was surprised that, now that we were married, Julian began treating me differently. He wanted a traditional housewife-type who would stay in, do the cooking and cleaning. Pick up dry-cleaning. Do laundry. Clean the cat litter. When I had enough published articles to quit my job to freelance, things got worse. Now that I was home all day, there were no excuses.

"It needs to look like the Four Seasons in here," he said.

I wondered what the obsession with hotels meant until I remembered he once told me that when he moved back to Mexico from Switzerland he and his mother lived in a hotel for a year. As an adult, he had a job that sent him to stay in five-star hotels throughout Latin America for business, and even when he was back in New York he liked to book rooms in the local fancy hotels for a night or two.

Julian still pulled a romantic surprise on occasion, and his latest was another hotel room, at the Millennium Hilton overlooking the disaster site of the World Trade Center. This time, he had two tablets of Ecstasy in his suit pocket. For old times' sake. We could take the feel-good truth drug and re-bond.

We took the pills and went to a bar called Circa Tabac, which sold cigarettes and was one of the few remaining places where you could smoke inside in New York City. We ordered Silk Cuts or Dunhills or some other European cigarettes. The smoke felt toxic as it entered my lungs. Julian decided to tell me the strange story about how things really ended with his last girlfriend, the one he took to Acapulco, the trip where he slammed against the rocks. They were still together months later, after I told Julian about Emir and he sent me the no-thanks email. She got pregnant. They decided to keep it. They began fighting all the time, hotheaded blowout arguments. While I was a quiet type who would do anything to keep the peace, she was more like Julian, aggressive. She probably stood up for herself whereas I quickly caved, cried, apologized, and begged forgiveness even during times when I knew I was in the right, and Julian respected me less for it. So they were having a huge fight in a bar, and she was four or so months along by then, showing, but not too much. She yelled back at him until her veins popped out, and then she began to bleed. She ran to the bathroom where, Julian said, she had a miscarriage.

If it weren't for that fight he wouldn't have been here with me. He would have been in a house in Greenwich, Connecticut or suburban New Jersey with her and their kid. It was one of the most depressing stories I'd ever heard. I wondered why he told it to me and why he chose that moment to do it. I wondered if maybe it wasn't true, if he was making it up to get a rise out of me. My trust and faith in him were dwindling. I knew that I shouldn't feel so scared and hurt all the time. I told myself the same thing Julian told me, that I was too sensitive. I'd seen this darker side of him now. No wonder he used to disappear for days on end—he had another part of himself he kept hidden. Married to him, I couldn't help seeing it. In marriage, there's nowhere to hide.

Back in the room towering over the construction site, Julian said, "You should cut your hair short. Really short."

"I like my hair long."

"You look so young. My colleagues think I'm married to a teenager."

"Won't that be a good thing down the line, when the other wives are getting plastic surgery and Botox and I still look like I'm in my twenties?"

"You should cut your hair really short. It wouldn't hurt to dress and act older, too. You wear the same kinds of clothes as in high school."

"And I still fit into them, too," I said under my breath, taking a dig at his increased weight.

Julian undressed as he spoke on about my immature tendencies. I listened from across the room in the dark. I felt confused. This was supposed to be the night we reconnected and got our relationship back into a positive place. It was turning into something else entirely. Why did he want to change me? He'd known me longer than Emir or anyone else in my life except my parents. We got into a bubble bath. I sat in front of him, his legs on either side of me. I tried to relax but everything suddenly felt off-kilter and disturbing, even the soft feel of his stomach against my back, the hairs on his chest tickling my shoulders. I realized I no longer felt safe with my husband. I thought about how much we changed since we were first together in high school and college. We had gone in different directions and weren't right for each other anymore. But this was marriage. I wasn't going to give up. A few days later, I had my long hair lopped off. I looked in the mirror. I looked as if I had aged five years in an hour but I convinced myself that it was sophisticated and mature and I liked it. I liked it because it made me closer to the kind of wife Julian wanted.

"Much better," he said when he came home from the office.

The first time Emir saw my new look, we met to try a new Thai place on Eighth Avenue.

"It's cute, but you said you'd never cut your long hair. What changed your mind?"

"I'm trying to look more professional," I said. "And, you know, I'm a married lady now."

Emir's eyes narrowed.

"Did Julian ask you to do this?"

"No," I said, with what I'm sure must have been a defensive edge in my voice. "He didn't ask."

I sought comfort in the fact that I could phrase this in such a way that I was not lying to Emir, at least not outright. Julian didn't ask. He demanded.

Emir looked unconvinced and I changed the subject. That I was hiding things from Emir should have tipped me off, but as it turned out, it took a lot more than that to get me to see how long I'd traveled on this road before realizing I'd made a wrong turn.

In December 2006, I received an email inviting me to a summer writing residency in Florida, from an organization that had bought and refurbished the house where Jack Kerouac lived when *On the Road* was published. The gift was a whole house for June, July, and August, all expenses paid. The residency came with an offer to teach a creative writing workshop, through Valencia Community College, in the Kerouac House living room. *Me, a college teacher?* I could hardly believe my good fortune.

"You can't go," Julian said. "You're married. You can't just take off."

I argued that it was Florida, a three-hour flight, and we could visit each other. Julian had weeks of vacation time accrued. He could unwind in the hammock out back while I wrote. He needed to unwind. We could go to Cocoa Beach for long weekends. Time to do nothing would be good for him and, for me, it was a huge honor to be asked to a prestigious residency in the former home of a writer I'd loved since I was fifteen. Julian used to be so supportive; what had changed? We went to a small Italian restaurant in the neighborhood to quietly talk it over, but Julian yelled at me about my selfishness in front of the whole room of intimate diners. When I cried, he apologized to the waiter for my behavior. "She's crazy," he said. "She's just crazy."

"I don't think I can go," I told Emir the next day.

"You have to," he said. "Especially now. You can't let him control your entire life. What's the next thing he's going to tell you that you 'can't' do? It sounds like Julian belongs in Emiristan! He'd be so at home there."

When I was married to Emir, I was flamboyant. With "the man of my dreams," I was shrinking, folding up inside myself, skittish and fearful.

"What changed in him?" I wondered aloud.

"He didn't change. There were parts of him you refused to see."

It hurt, but I knew Emir was right, and was glad there was

one person I could count on to always be completely honest, even when he knew it wasn't what I would want to hear.

I finished my first novel before I left for Orlando, and a publisher wanted it. I got the call while at one of my freelance jobs, as a research editor at my favorite magazine, *Jane*. It was the happiest day. Fights with Julian had been worsening. During another he said, "Your father was basically a sperm donor," and I ran from the apartment wishing I could melt into the floor. But that night we celebrated. He took me to Buddha Bar, bought champagne, and congratulated me. I hoped it was all going to work out, that we would get through our rough patch. I wrote to my father and shared the news. Several weeks later he hadn't written back, and though I knew something was wrong it was easy to pretend it wasn't because this was normal.

When I got to the house in Orlando, I missed Julian painfully at first. I stared at the words on the screen and broke down, worried I had sabotaged our marriage, and for what? Why did I need to do this? But as the quiet days wore on and I revised the novel, I began to feel a sense of peace I hadn't realized had been missing. My stomach wasn't clenched all the time. My regular eczema breakouts cleared up. At twenty-seven I had just turned the corner into the career I dreamed of yet thought impossible: as a professional writer with a first novel about to be published. When Julian planned a trip to come down for his birthday, I was excited to see him. I knew things were going to be different now that we'd had some space and could reconnect.

True to form, he booked a room in a luxury hotel, in Miami. The night of July 7th, we went with a small group—Julian's work colleague and my Orlando writing friend JC and his then-girlfriend, Sarah—to a club called Cameo. Bottle after bottle arrived at our table. I had a few glasses of champagne. I wasn't keeping track of how much Julian drank but I did notice it was a lot. We got back to the hotel around four in the morning. Everyone dispersed. Julian and I entered our room. And that's when he turned into someone I had never seen before, not even when he was at his angriest. He was in a blackout, ranting like a madman that he was going to call my grandmother and tell her all about how terrible I really was, how in spite of his efforts against it a certain motherfucker had been allowed to stay in the country.

Even after an anonymous tip.

"I didn't tell you there was an anonymous phone call."

Julian came closer. I could smell his hot bourbon breath.

"You did."

He towered over me in the small white room.

"No. I didn't."

I had the thought that he could kill me so easily, even by accident, that he wasn't himself. He was angry, threatening, verging on violent. I cowered, my eyes darting around the room, my mind automatically mapping the escape route to the door. If he grabbed me, if it turned physical, I would be completely at his mercy.

"You just want to fuck a gay guy," he said. I was assessing

the possibility of exiting through the window, which opened directly onto the ground-floor patio. He reached for my laptop on the table. I knew what he was going to do. All my work was on that laptop. I should never have come here. This was a mistake.

I don't remember how I caught it as it left his hands on its way across the room, where it would have smashed against the wall, but the next thing I knew, I had the laptop in my arms and was running barefoot down the outdoor hallway to security.

The security guard went back to the room and got my purse for me. He came back with the purse and Julian behind him, saying something about how he'd seen the guard at the club that night. "That's impossible, sir," the guard said. "I've been on my shift since five." He handed me my purse. I walked outside, got in a taxi, and asked the driver to take me to the airport, where I bought a flight back to Orlando, went back to the residency house, cried, and slept until three in the afternoon, when Julian showed up at the door. He apologized and asked what happened. He said he would get help and never drink again. I thought about my father.

Trying to destroy my writing was trying to destroy the largest part of my identity. Had he succeeded, Julian would have smashed the physical, external representation of the one thing I was proud of; I had dreamed since childhood of growing up to be a writer and, as anyone with a true dream does, I worked hard and at all costs to make it happen. There couldn't be a fallback plan and I didn't have a backup drive. The laptop and the words saved on it were that little girl's dream.

In one of my earliest memories, my father stumbles into my room in the middle of the night, yelling in Italian. He and

my mother fight after he gets home from working at the restaurant. He is drunk. I'm taking an art class for little kids. I'd
brought home my first sculpture that week, a wire sculpture
implanted in white clay we had made ourselves. Wire affixed to
clay affixed to a piece of driftwood. I'm proud of the sculpture
and display it on my dresser. My father picks it up and hurtles it
across the room. It shatters against the wall.

When I returned to New York in August, I packed some suitcases and went to Emir's. Julian had moved to New Jersey by
then, a subletter in the Chelsea apartment. Emir helped me
scour Craigslist for a few hours, and we went to look at a
six-month sublet a few blocks from the apartment he shared
with Stan in the East Village. I paid a deposit on the room. It
took another three months of painful back-and-forth before I
decided that a second divorce was the right choice. I could not
go back to a man who tried to hurt me that way. I'd made the
very marriage mistake I dreaded, the one I married Emir in an
effort to try to avoid, and it wasn't the end of everything as I
had once thought divorce surely would be. It was Emir who
was there for me when what was supposed to be my "real"
marriage ended. He seemed to know it was coming, but he
didn't say anything about that. Instead, he offered me all the
comforts one gives a brokenhearted friend—hugs, cups of tea,
a listening ear, cocktails, mac and cheese—though his presence
alone was sufficient.

Who was Julian? Had I ever really known? Why did I expect
us—why was I so determined for us—to succeed? I still did not

know how to be a partner, or a wife, or maybe we just weren't right for each other after all.

There were other signs, signs I was less willing to see: our wedding ceremony in a dead language, neither of us facing each other, both facing the ocean. The unknown, the abyss. We said no vows, made no promises. Both times he proposed, he slid the ring on my finger in the dark, taking the decision-making agency away from me, and I never minded because there was no decision to make. When it came to Julian the answer was always yes.

Do we know what is inevitable or do we lead inevitability into being with the amount of energy we focus on what we fear? It turned out to be the same starter marriage it would have been, had we gone through with it when I was twenty-one. He became controlling and I withdrew.

Seeing Emir as a lesson in marriage had been naïve, and being certain that by divorcing him I'd fulfill some sort of quota that guaranteed I'd go on to be happily married for life was indeed magical thinking. I was looking for the storybook ending, the breaking of an imaginary curse I had mistaken for real all along. This was messy, imperfect, ironic, miraculous life.

Though Julian and I were married for three years, his green card still wasn't finalized. The one predictable thing in life may be that this process—INS, DHS, WTF—crawls along at a snail's pace. Julian met me on a street corner in Manhattan and begged me not to file until the green card was finalized.

"Please don't have me kicked out of the country," he said.

I granted him that wish. We stayed married for a year after we separated so Julian's status in the country would not be jeopardized. We lived apart and didn't speak to each other anymore. The situation was in direct opposition to staying married an extra year to Emir *after* he got his green card and sharing a home just because we liked the way things were. The Julian-divorce was the opposite of the Emir-divorce in every way: long, ugly, brutal. Our lawyers argued across the table while Julian argued with them both. I sat in uncomfortable silence and let the lawyer do whatever talking was left.

Marriage to Emir, which began with his need for the green card, became, like the Velveteen Rabbit, more real with love and wear. Emir remains one of the most important people in my life. The marriage to Julian, which sprang from romantic love, turned into a green card arrangement with no relationship. In the end, the "fake" marriage was more "real" than the "real" one.

Emir's relationship with Stan was growing more serious. Emir was getting tired of lying to his father, saying he lived with a roommate, "just some guy." He made one of the biggest decisions of his life. He decided to come out to his father. That it was going to happen on a visit to Emiristan rather than over the phone freaked me out.

His father was steering the car toward the airport to drop Emir off at the end of the visit when Emir told him, at the last possible moment, that he was gay and lived with his boyfriend. He told Mohammad at the airport curb, surrounded by security and right before Emir would make an easy escape up into the sky, back to New York, where he would be safe.

His father refused to believe him at first—it must be a joke, there is no such thing, no son of his—and then, when Moham- mad did decide to believe Emir, he refused to speak to him. It would be a year before he came around, to a place of greater, though not total, acceptance. I was proud of Emir for what he'd done. I'd never been able to have an honest confrontation with my father about our secrets, and Emir had taken the ultimate risk that required so much courage on his part and could have ended in circumstances I did not want to imagine.

Emir's younger sister, Soraya, became famous in Emiristan. She didn't set out to become an actress; she was "discovered," plucked by a casting agent for an ice cream commercial.

One thing led to another and the next thing Soraya al- Habibi knew, she was starring in movies and television shows and working on her English in anticipation of a Hollywood crossover. This got Emir a lot of attention in his country; he was written up in newspapers and magazines as "Soraya's screen- writer brother in New York." Emir wrote a script for Soraya to star in and his American dream found international success. "What really attracts me are stories told by flawed characters," he is quoted as saying in an interview.

When I first met Soraya, she was just a kid, and now that she was older, she began to take the place in Emir's life that had once been reserved for me. She used to be jealous of me, Emir once told me, and now the reverse was true.

At Soraya's latest movie premiere, Emir brought Stan and they walked down the red carpet together. Emir told Mohammad he was coming back for the premiere, and they didn't have to see each other if Mohammad didn't want to. If he did want to see his son, though, he would have to agree to meet Stan, and to treat them both graciously.    Mohammad wasn't happy about it, but he was cordial. He was neither going to accept them nor have them killed. In 2007 things were changing. Mohammad did not approve of Soraya's acting career either but he attended her premiere and stood by supportively. Mohammad would never embrace his son's sexuality as my mother would never love that I'd married my friend to keep him in the country, but neither wielded the same power over us as they had when we were twenty-two. They were no longer larger-than-life, authoritative people. They were just people and we just happened to exist because of them.

"It wasn't a relaxing vacation," Emir said when he got back to New York.

Though Mohammad shook Stan's hand and had dinner with the couple, he later pulled Emir aside and told him that he would be glad when "this phase" was over. We'd had the conversation many times—the impossibility of his father ever accepting him or believing that his sexuality was not a choice he was making to be defiant.

On July 7th, 2008—Julian's birthday, the one-year anniversary of the night in the Miami hotel room, the night I fled in fear from his rage—I rode the ferry out to Fire Island, to a town called Cherry Grove, where my friends—a couple, Glenn and Jeffrey—had rented a beach house for the week. Since July 7th had become a dreaded day, I wanted to spend it in a peaceful setting. Walking on the sand and swimming in the ocean in the company of a laid-back couple was for me the best way to both reflect and escape.

It was a beautiful day on Fire Island, sun peeking through clouds, mountainous waves undulating, building in force, rising, and crashing on the hard sand of the shore. Glenn and I took a long walk on the beach. A journalist, Glenn was working on a memoir about family, sexuality, and an awkward coming of age, so we often shared stories of our work and the challenges it presented. That day, I asked Glenn if his father's recent death had changed the story, or its ending, and if he planned to incorporate it into the book.

"I don't know," he said, staring off at the horizon, his cheeks already pinked from the sun. "I'm feeling torn about it. I'm not sure yet if I'll put it in."

I suggested he end it with his father still alive—an upbeat note. He would give that some thought, he said. At sunset, Glenn, Jeffrey, and I ate pizza slices and they walked me to the ferry. I thanked them for a wonderful day. On the ferry ride home, the bars on my phone leapt to life. Voicemail after voicemail beeped in. They were all from my mother. She sounded panicked. *I'll try you again*, each one said. *I'm going to try you again.* From her tone and lack of the singsong *hiiii Liiiiiize*, it was clear something was wrong. I couldn't call her back. I had no international calling card on me. I stared at the phone, willing it to ring. I was on the train by the time it did. It was already dark and my fluorescent-lit reflection stared back at me through the window glass. I answered on the first ring and she told me my father was dead. My body tensed. My throat felt hollowed out. I could barely get out, *when?*

It didn't come out until the following week that he had actually died five days before, on July 2nd. It took five days to find out as my father's estranged younger brother was traveling with his wife when my father slipped into a coma back in Genoa. He drank himself to death. It was advanced alcoholic cirrhosis of the liver and that was what killed him, though I suppose it's fair to say he killed himself.

When I got home, I lay on the carpet and cried.

My father couldn't make it to my milestone days—graduations or the wedding—and then he was dead and I couldn't make it to his funeral. There was no way to get there on time; even if I'd boarded the next flight to Italy, it would have been over before I arrived. We'd been locked in this father–daughter dance of avoidance for twenty-two years, and still I expected a surprise ending, a cinematic twist: our final scene running toward each other on a crowded street in an Italian city.

That I didn't go to my father's funeral still haunts me. Situations in which you cannot get closure retain an unfinished quality. The closure must become that very lack of closure; it must become the ability of a person to accept that, to grow stronger, to know that there was nothing you could have done to make things otherwise, any other way than the outcome that occurred. Or at least this is the only kind of thought that assuages the pain of such loss, even the loss of an absence, the double negative—even several years later.

When my father died, I was left to grieve the absence of an absence. The Lack. He wasn't communicative and his death only removed the possibility of future communication. I dreamed of him, though. In the dream, he was swimming with dolphins. He said it was beautiful there. My father had only once before appeared in a dream. I was standing on a wooden bridge in a frozen landscape, everything covered in ice and snow. My father pointed down at the frozen river the bridge traversed. I looked. Beneath the ice, in the stillness, were bright orange koi fish, unmoving, frozen.

"There are poems down there," the dream father says.

It was no revelation that the unresolved bothered me more than anything—that I had often behaved as if having the facts alone could lead to some kind of transcendence, or at least a vague sense of relief. I wondered whether keeping secrets to protect someone you love was okay. Was it harmful, beneficial, both? It seemed an unanswerable question. My mother and I had both tried to protect each other from truths we feared would cause the other suffering, difficult truths we each decided the other would be better off not knowing. I wished I had been told, so that I would have had some agency in deciding what action to take—if any—about my father, and the removal of choice made me feel she'd betrayed me. But she also may have made the best decision for me. If I had told her about my marriage to Emir before we went to Vegas, she would have tried to talk me out of it, or threatened to report us to get me not to go through with it. If I told her after we tied the knot she would have demanded an annulment and, when I refused, spent the next two years worrying and obsessing about the possible consequences. Secrecy was a protective shroud. I still don't know the answer to the question of whether either one of us was right in how we handled the situations.

I would also never get any closer to finding out whether any of the scenes I imagined in my head held any truth, whether my father fell down in the marketplace, or died in the apartment and hadn't been found for four days, whether he vomited blood and checked himself into the hospital, and his estranged brother had thought it best I not see him in that condition. Maybe he was right, and being left to imagine was better than having some horrible image seared into my memory.

Later, I would tell Glenn to disregard that advice I gave him that day on the beach. If you're telling stories about your father and he dies before you finish the book it seems dishonest to omit it, as if you could write your present from a place of your past.

For two more years I imagined the day I would visit my father's grave, our long-overdue reunion. I would sit on the grass by the gravestone, which I imagined to be in a quaint old cemetery on a hill overlooking the sea in Genoa, and talk to my father or the lack of him. I still haven't been.

On some level, I had wanted to save my father, or at least to believe that I could, though I already knew this was impossible. Every relationship I entered, Emir included, invoked my impulse to save, to rescue, to shelter. I couldn't do it for my father, for Emir, or for anyone. It wasn't my role or my place. My father kept me at a distance, as if he knew it would not be right to fully let me in given his condition. His alcoholism was the elephant, the dark other that loomed over us, wedged itself between us, and kept us forever and truly apart. By marrying Emir I was playing out my parents' marriage in certain ways, without the sex so I could maintain a certain distance, a cool remove, as if that might piece back together what was broken.

July 8th, the day after I found out about my father's death, Emir and I had a long-standing appointment. I booked us treatments at a downtown spa on Great Jones Street, my gift to him for his thirtieth birthday three months earlier and to celebrate his latest screenplay placing in the finalists of an international competition. The timing of this pampering seemed as fitting as it did wrong. Though I had made the appointment months before, I felt guilty for lounging away, getting a massage and facial at an expensive spa during a time of mourning. As if the universe itself agreed with my initial assumption, an email from the Italian consulate popped up on my phone during a break between the massage and the facial, instructing me to proceed to their offices as soon as possible. Some forms had arrived regarding transferring my father's estate—debt—from my responsibility to his brother's. The forms needed my signature.

My mother had made it clear that it was urgent I sign them the day the consulate had them ready, as the debt was accruing and the estranged uncle wanted to pay as soon as possible, which was as soon as he received the forms. I forced my own delusions aside—that my father had been secretly wealthy and his brother was trying to steal the money, that I had a huge inheritance, that Papa had been the *Marchese di Monferrato* after all. I told Emir I had to leave the spa for the consulate immediately to get the forms signed and off to Italy before the end of the business day.

"You stay and get your facial," I said. "I'll go."

"Are you kidding? I'm coming with you."

We'd been each other's date to every bureaucratic office in the past, Emir said. We had a tradition to uphold. Really, he just didn't want me to be alone.

"Five years after our divorce, you're still the best husband."

"You need me. Of course I am going to be here for you."

Emir and I changed and got our things from the locker room, then met back out in the spa's lobby. We hailed a taxi on the curb and I gave the driver the cross streets for the Italian consulate on Park Avenue. I had met the consul there before, when I had gone a year earlier to renew my Italian passport. His name was also Giovanni.

The receptionist signed us in and told us to head upstairs. Emir followed me up the winding marble staircase of the beautiful old mansion.

Consul-Giovanni said he was so sorry to hear of Father-Giovanni's passing, and slid the forms across the desk. I sat down in a maroon leather chair.

I signed the forms and Consul-Giovanni stamped them. Stamped them again. Stamped. Again. Another. Stamp-stamp. Stamp. Among the many stories my father used to tell me about his former life, before my mother came to Italy, one of his favorites was about the country's notoriously slow, overly complicated, and stamp-ridden bureaucracy—getting a license, his hospitality school degree, identification, credentials—the point was always about how this ubiquitous and bordering on compulsive stamping of documents was virtually a national pastime. He had joked about how long it took to get anything done because every piece of paperwork, no matter how trivial it seemed, needed a deluge of stamps in order to be considered official. I must have been around nine or ten years old, and I listened, giggling occasionally at the funny parts, balancing my elbows on the white dining table a few feet from his Murphy bed in his Seattle studio apartment, my chin pressing down between my palms.

Consul-Giovanni finished stamping the forms and handed them back to me. Emir and I thanked him as we stood to go. Giovanni walked us down the hallway to the elevator, kissed me on each cheek as was Italian custom, and offered his condolences again. Then he turned to Emir and placed a hand on his shoulder.

"You take good care of her, okay?"

Emir was sworn in as a citizen of the United States of America eight years after we promised Elvis we would walk our hound dogs and polish our blue suede shoes. Emir threw a citizenship party in the gay porn studio's loft. I made a red, white, and blue flag-shaped cake. It was too sweet but Emir ate a big slice anyway. There were streamers and the stereo blasted Elvis (and Liza) all night. The theme was "American Icons."

I thought our story could find an endpoint after that, but there was more.

The economy collapsed. Architecture was hit hard. Emir's partner, Stan, a South African citizen, was laid off, his H-1B visa gone the way of the job that sponsored it. Around the same time, the owner of the gay porn studio who kept Emir on his health insurance plan announced he was moving the company back to his native Germany. Emir's health insurance went away. His doctor advised him not to go off a prescription medication he had been taking. El Toro came to the interim rescue, sending the drug from Canada.

Then Emir confessed they might be moving there.

Stan couldn't find another job to sponsor his visa. I couldn't believe Emir's partner was in the same situation Emir had found himself in back in 2001, when I'd offered to marry him. If they moved to Montreal, Emir could get any prescription medication he needed and Stan could start his own architecture firm or more easily get authorized to work freelance.

And they could get married.

El Toro said it had been easy to start up his own business there, an arts management firm. I was aghast that after years of jumping through fire-ringed hoops in a bureaucratic circus and finally reaching the pot of gold—citizenship—Emir had to choose between his partner and his country, like a love triangle.

So many people must be in this predicament, I thought, and I wondered why there wasn't more public outrage about it. I didn't want Emir to go, but even more so, the idea of a choice between the person you love and the place you've made your home shook me to the core. Emir didn't want to leave, either, but his lack of health insurance combined with Stan's visa crisis meant there might not be a choice, and Canada was the closest place to New York they could feasibly go. Or Johannesburg, Stan's home city, where same-sex couples can also marry.

"If only we could here," Emir said. "Nothing's going to happen until it becomes federal."

"Can't Stan marry an American and stay?" I asked.

Seven years later, I was still at it.

"Stan doesn't have a friend like you," Emir said.

"Want me to do it?"

We laughed because we both knew that this time I wasn't serious. I liked Stan very much, both as a friend and because he was a solid long-term partner to Emir. But I didn't love him that way, and we both knew it was a ridiculous idea.

Last resort: my mother. Seven years later and I was still at that, too.

This was proving to be not a period of my life but rather its unending circumstance. I wanted my mother to retire so that something would change. If she didn't work for the government anymore, her authority and investment in the system would evaporate and for the first time she could be nothing but Mom, though she would never stop being Profiler Mom.

I explained Stan's visa problem, which mirrored the visa problem Emir first encountered eight years before.

"Is there anything else they can do besides move to another country?" I asked, expecting the same spiel about Canada having an easier immigration process, a more lax system—and that the options were either the H-1B via employer sponsorship, or asylum. But this time my mother surprised me.

"Emir should be a test case," she said.

"What does that mean?"

"If Emir and Stan got married in a state where gay marriage is legal, Emir could file the paperwork to immigrate his spouse."

"But Ma, DOMA is still federal law, no?"

"That's why it's a test case. Emir tries to put the paperwork through, it gets denied because they are gay, he sues the government for discrimination, and then it goes all the way to the Supreme Court, where he historically wins federal marriage rights for gays."

"Are you kidding me?"

"Now that he's a U.S. citizen, he should at least try."

"Yeah, our newest second-class citizen. Welcome to America!"

"Listen, Lize. What I'm saying is, he should do that—get the media involved, go out and try to change things."

The media—of course. She would love to see Emir's face on the news, making history. I could finally have my three minutes in the spotlight, too. When does one pick up a cause randomly, as if thumbing through a phone book: *Civil rights? Welfare reform? Domestic violence?* We get involved in what we are connected to, like recovering alcoholics counseling other recovering alcoholics. The common thread is vested interest.

One week before Stan's H-1B was set to expire, the week before Canada, something of a miracle happened. Out of hundreds of applications, Stan got a job at a two-person architecture firm. Emir and I made plans to meet for lunch to celebrate, and I waited for him in the small park off the Christopher Street subway station on a warm early spring day. I had old memories of places now. Places had context. And the ability to haunt me.

I texted him when I got there: *im in the square now between the statue and the homeless guy.* I spotted him through the small trees, watching as if he were a rare and exotic creature that one must sit still for hours in the brush, hoping to glimpse. After all these years, I'm still amazed by him. That afternoon, Emir wore faded jeans, a moss-green shirt, and his aviator sunglasses. He had a new, shorter haircut and looked handsome. I ran out of the park and called his name. He ran to me. We hugged.

"You know there are like ten statues and twenty homeless guys," he said into my ear and we laughed. Sometimes I could hear the word "homeless" and not automatically think of my father.

We went to Philip Marie on Hudson Street and sat at a table in the sun. It was spring and the people of the West Village were getting puppies. We pointed out the cute little pugs and bichon frises to each other. When the server came we ordered the same: Salade Niçoise and lemonades. We talked about love, sex, monogamy, and whether or not open relationships were a better idea than cheating. Over lemonade, I told Emir the one regret I had about the time we were married was that I moved out when I did. "That whole apartment thing," I called it. It was a mistake. I regretted it.

"We could have stayed like that forever," he said. "Together. We had a safe bubble. We had to put ourselves out there."

With Emir and me one thing was certain. If anything could have destroyed us, it would have been the marriage, but the marriage, in the end, brought us closer. If we hadn't spent those years together we might have lost each other as we had drifted away from so many friends over the years. Instead we became family. The check came and as Emir reached for his wallet I noticed we had the same book in our bags. I pulled out my copy of *The Anatomy of Story.* "Look," I said. We laughed. After marriages, divorces, lovers, recessions, immigration troubles, some dreams achieved and others abandoned, our connection is still "'til death do us part."

Whatever Emir and I had been, continued to be—partners, outlaws, an exercise in consciousness, a case study—was not for me to decide or the story to tell. Whoever I meet, whatever happens next, Emir will always be the one, the happily ever after. He freed me to move forward, with an ever-present link to a common past.

Sometimes I am forced to think of Julian because we have mutual friends on Facebook. This is how it is now. Sometimes I wonder about asking how he's doing, but I know better. The Lack is there, but I see that incompletion also can be beautiful. The Japanese concept of Wabi-Sabi explores this notion by removing transience from the realm of unfortunate things and turning it into something to be celebrated. Wabi-Sabi embraces imperfection. Rather than looking at home as a place to seek out on a massive quest or as a man I was absolutely fated to be with, I could instead take hold of the idea of home as something that was already mine, that had been all along. It was all around me. As for marriage—nothing is truly permanent, but I wasn't doomed when it came to love because of my parents. That was an excuse or an illusion. I could try again at some point, or not. Either way, I've stopped trying to make predictions about relationships, with one exception.

Emir and I will have each other for as long as we both shall live, no matter what, no strings attached, no questions asked. Maybe, to see how this plays out, we'll create a joint Twitter account and you can follow us. We've grown apart a thousand times and come back together twice as often. I'm surprised by the malleability of some relationships. We've stuck it out. It's a relationship I can count on for life, enough to write it down, to put it out there, the closet be damned. At some point in our lives, we all have to come out about something.

I still believe in marriage. I still think it's fundamentally a good idea, a solid institution that any couple should be able to enter into. I would do it again.

It is 2011 and I'm writing these lines from the couch in Emir's living room—the nobody knows i'm gay magnet on the fridge, the posters on the walls. Emir sits at his desk, typing away on his latest screenplay. Every time we have one of these work dates, we occasionally break to talk, usually offering progress reports about our writing, or to ask for feedback on what we're working on. Sometimes, we read aloud to each other.

We had many discussions surrounding "the book about us," and reflecting on our friendship for its purposes.

But then he said this:

"Sex is not what makes a relationship a relationship. It's someone who challenges and supports you, and makes willing sacrifices. It's someone you're willing to go on an unknown journey with, like when we moved here together. It's about consistency, support systems, and trust established. In school, we established our relationship, but not that trust, that came later, when we were married. By the end we were in this place couples dream of getting to. Living out the meaning of the marriage vows didn't happen at the wedding, it happened after that. We became more vulnerable to each other. How much of your vulnerable side are you willing to show someone else? People come of age in different ways, and we were so young, both coming of age together. You're still the first person I tell things to. Like a shrink."

Of course, I thought. In the end, Emir said it better than I ever could. Sometimes I envied his ability to spontaneously phrase things exactly right.

He continued on. "When I was getting cereal I saw a fridge magnet of mine. It's a quote by 'Unknown.' You probably saw it before."

"NOBODY KNOWS I'M GAY?"

"You were always so obsessed by that stupid magnet. I'm talking about the other magnet, the one right next to it."

*Another magnet?* I never noticed another magnet. NOBODY KNOWS dominated the fridge, at least it did for me. I remembered that it had once been *my* magnet; I can't remember how it came to be in my possession. Maybe this magnet was the only one I chose to see. Perhaps my fixation on it was to the detriment of all the other quotable magnets.

We see what we want to see.

"What does it say?" I asked.

"It says 'Everything will be okay in the end. If it's not okay, it's not the end.'"

## Afterword

In August 2013, after twenty-one years, Anthony Makk and Bradford Wells had their relationship officially recognized by the U.S. Government. Makk received his green card the week after the couple's spousal interview at the U.S. Citizenship and Immigration Services' (formerly the INS) San Francisco Field Office.

Immigration Equality filed their spousal green card petition in 2011. Their application was initially denied because of DOMA, but House Democratic Leader Nancy Pelosi and Senator Dianne Feinstein intervened and secured Makk a two-year "deferred action." With DOMA repealed and the green card secured, the married couple no longer needs to rely on temporary stays of deportation.

Makk and Wells now live in San Francisco.

Also in August 2013, Emir walked me down the aisle for the third time—this time with my mother beside us, too—to give me away at my Northern California wedding to my beloved Jason. In addition to being a loving, caring, supportive, wonderful, totally real husband who makes me feel lucky every day, he is a U.S. citizen, so we didn't have to worry about the green card.

# Acknowledgments

It was a six-year journey from first to final draft, and as I mentioned in Chapter 17, working for a literary agent when I first lived in New York at twenty-two, I came to understand "all the hands that went into making a book." Well, I have countless hands to thank for their help during the time I was realizing this one. Any omissions are unintentional, so if I forgot you please throw a drink in my face the next time we run into each other. Or, better yet, I'll buy you one.

Deepest thanks to:
My agent, Jennifer Lyons—impossible without you. You have gone above and beyond on a million occasions. And to Charlie for pointing me in her direction, I'll always be grateful.

My editor, Dan Smetanka at Soft Skull/Counterpoint, for all of his thoughtful expertise. His careful work made this a better book. Megan Fishmann, Liz Parker, Emma Cofod, and the rest of the team at Soft Skull/Counterpoint for their dedication and enthusiasm for this project and tireless contributions to making it a success.

Delia Casa, for help nailing the subtitle, and coming through when I most needed someone to believe in me. I hope our paths will cross again.

Michael Cendejas and his team at the Lynn Pleshette Agency for their work on the mysterious Hollywood side of things.

The Kerouac Project of Orlando, where this book was truly born, even if I only salvaged about twelve lines from that 400-page first draft. Thanks Bob Kealing, Mike Robinson, Kim Buchheit, Summer Rodman, Steven McCall, Ilyse Kusnetz, Brad Kuhn, Darlyn Finch, Joseph Hayes, Jennifer Greenhill-Taylor, Patrick Greene, Urban ReThink, Stardust Video & Coffee (where, in addition to the Kerouac House, many, many pages were written), the magic of the Kerouac house, Spanish moss, lizards doing push-ups, and the little pineapple that grew in the backyard. Extra thanks to Kim for her beautiful photos and the return to Vegas.

Columbia University's MFA program, where I had the opportunity to workshop my shitty first draft into workable form. Thank you to the incredible faculty I had the pleasure to work with: Leslie Sharpe, Stephen O'Connor, Patty O'Toole, Phillip Lopate, Richard Locke, Lis Harris, Amy Benson, Nicole Wallack, Jonathan Lethem, Lynne Sharon Schwartz, and Oliver Sacks. Thank you colleagues, and friends who came together around various workshop and restaurant tables: Jeramey Kraatz, Kassi Underwood, Liz Greenwood, Emily Feder, Nell Boeschenstein, Leah Carroll, Tana Wojczuk, Matthew Parker,

Bridget Potter, Harvest Henderson, Lindsay Harrison, Liz Topp, Meg Winter, Catherine Lacey, Emily Adler, Sean Madigan Hoen, Rachel Riederer, Kyle Valenta, Maggie Sowell, Anna Spiegel, Julie Cohen, Akiva Freidlin, Astri von Arbin Ahlander, Jobie Hughes, Deenah Vollmer, Abby Rabinowitz, Alexis Tonti, Starre Vartan, Vanessa Hartmann, Mike Spies, Suzanne Mozes, Gila Lyons, Rachel Ghansah, Ryan Kearney, Daniella Gitlin, Mike Shea—to those I've lost touch with since, I'm still very grateful to you.

Glenn Michael Gordon, for eight years (and counting) of friendship and sharing our work—you always say the thing that makes the difference.

Sherene Schostak, for many hours helping me excavate.

Emerson College: thanks especially to Mary Ann Cicala, Tori Weston, Tikesha R. Morgan, and Chris Serwacki for bringing me back on occasion. Thanks to EAGLE, the Castle, the L.A. program, and WLP. I could not be more proud to call Emerson my alma mater.

Thank you to the Thurber House in Columbus, Ohio—where it was an honor to be the inaugural John E. Nance Writer-in-Residence, and to finish this book in Thurber's home. Thank you Sally Crane, Susanne Jaffe, Anne Touvel, Erin Deel, Meg Brown, and Katie Poole for such a magical, life-changing month. Thank you Kimmel Harding Nelson Center for the Arts in Nebraska City: Jenni Brant, Pat Friedli, and the December '12 artists, who made the residency productive and great. Thanks, Angie Rovetto, for afternoons at Vetto's.

Thank you to early readers, teachers, and dear ones: Em, amazing husband, perfect friend, incredible creative mind. Thank you for reading endless drafts and giving me so many detailed notes, for aiding me with your perspective, and for coming to my rescue in many situations. Josie McGee, JC Sevcik, and Melynda Fuller provided crucial feedback at critical junctures. Penina Roth, for the Franklin Park Reading Series, friendship, and support. Thank you to Andy Devlin for the handmade first edition. Susan Shapiro, thank you for being my first mentor and second mother. Writer friends Jen Cacicio, Sarah Greene, Heather Kristin, Felicia Sullivan, and Sarah Rainone for your always-wise insights and friendship. Teachers Daphne Merkin and Nick Flynn, whose workshops pushed me further into the unknown. Michael Seidenberg, for Brazen Head times and more. Kat Kaller, Shara Richter, Michelle Alcala, Helen Neiman, and Brandon Ruiz—thank you, friends.

Editors and fellow writers I have had the pleasure to work with in various contexts: ongoing thanks to Cindy Spiegel, Daniel Jones, Paula Derrow, Rebecca Walker, Sarah Hepola, Sari Botton, Alex Garinger, Kim Perel and Wendy Sherman, Jessamine Chan, Mark Rotella, Parul Sehgal, Leah Odze Epstein, and Caren Osten Gerszberg.

Thanks to my students past and present, who inspire and motivate me, and to the organizations that allow me to teach: Columbia University's Undergraduate Writing Program, UCLA Extension: Linda Venis, Katy Flaherty, Alicia Wheeler;

University of California Santa Cruz—Kresge College: Micah Perks and Juan Poblete; and the Mediabistro.com team.

I never imagined I'd find a soul mate before this book was finished. Thank you to my husband Jason: my dream come true, greatest collaborator, love of my life, who arrived just in time to help me proofread, and whose suggestions are always spot-on. Thanks to my Mom, The Profiler, for making herself available for research, and for saying "if you get arrested, it will be great publicity for your book." I could not have been the writer I am without you. Grandma, Amy, and all the Scheinmans and Gennatiempos out there. My Warehouse family, I feel blessed to be one of you.

And to Raízes do Brazil Capoeira for reminding me near daily of all those other parts of me south of the brain, for the introduction to too many friends to name here (not to mention the husband), and for teaching me I'm capable of things I didn't think I could do (anything remotely acrobatic, singing in public, etc).

Thank you to readers and booksellers for keeping literature alive.